OPPOSING
VIEWPOINTS®
SERIES

# Cosmetic Surgery

# Other Books of Related Interest:

**Opposing Viewpoints Series**

Celebrity Culture

Male and Female Roles

The Culture of Beauty

**At Issue Series**

Beauty Pageants

Body Piercing and Tatoos

How Far Should Science Extend the Human Lifespan?

**Current Controversies Series**

Medical Ethics

The Elderly

"Congress shall make no law ... abridging the freedom of speech, or of the press."

*First Amendment to the U.S. Constitution*

The basic foundation of our democracy is the First Amendment guarantee of freedom of expression. The Opposing Viewpoints Series is dedicated to the concept of this basic freedom and the idea that it is more important to practice it than to enshrine it.

**OPPOSING VIEWPOINTS® SERIES**

# Cosmetic Surgery

*Roman Espejo, Book Editor*

**GREENHAVEN PRESS**
*A part of Gale, Cengage Learning*

GALE
CENGAGE Learning™

Detroit • New York • San Francisco • New Haven, Conn • Waterville, Maine • London

GALE
CENGAGE Learning

Christine Nasso, *Publisher*
Elizabeth Des Chenes, *Managing Editor*

© 2011 Greenhaven Press, a part of Gale, Cengage Learning

Gale and Greenhaven Press are registered trademarks used herein under license.

*For more information, contact:*
Greenhaven Press
27500 Drake Rd.
Farmington Hills, MI 48331-3535
Or you can visit our Internet site at gale.cengage.com

For product information and technology assistance, contact us at

Gale Customer Support, 1-800-877-4253
For permission to use material from this text or product, submit all requests online at www.cengage.com/permissions

Further permissions questions can be emailed to permissionrequest@cengage.com

Articles in Greenhaven Press anthologies are often edited for length to meet page requirements. In addition, original titles of these works are changed to clearly present the main thesis and to explicitly indicate the author's opinion. Every effort is made to ensure that Greenhaven Press accurately reflects the original intent of the authors. Every effort has been made to trace the owners of copyrighted material.

Cover image Jupiterimages/Getty Images.

LIBRARY OF CONGRESS CATALOGING-IN-PUBLICATION DATA

Cosmetic surgery / Roman Espejo, book editor.
    p. cm. -- (Opposing viewpoints)
Includes bibliographical references and index.
ISBN 978-0-7377-4958-8 (hardcover) -- ISBN 978-0-7377-4959-5 (pbk.)
1. Surgery, Plastic--Popular works. I. Espejo, Roman, 1977-
RD119.C6816 2011
617.9'5--dc22

                                                              2010039234

Printed in the United States of America
1 2 3 4 5 6 7 15 14 13 12 11

# Contents

Why Consider Opposing Viewpoints?                     11

Introduction                                          14

## Chapter 1: Is Cosmetic Surgery Safe?

Chapter Preface                                       18

1. Cosmetic Surgery Is Safe                           20
   *California Health and Beauty*

2. Cosmetic Surgery Is Dangerous                      25
   *Jenny Kleeman*

3. Cosmetic Surgery Tourism Is Safe                   34
   *John Otis*

4. Cosmetic Surgery Tourism Is Dangerous              40
   *Victoria Corderi*

Periodical Bibliography                               49

## Chapter 2: Who Should Have Cosmetic Surgery?

Chapter Preface                                       51

1. Cosmetic Surgery Can Benefit Some Teens            53
   *Richard D'Amico, as told to Matthew Shulman*

2. Teens Should Not Have Cosmetic Surgery             59
   *Sabrina Joseph and Khorally Pierre*

3. Ethnic Characteristics Should Be Considered        64
   Prior to Cosmetic Surgery
   *Amy Wilentz*

4. People Who Seek Plastic Surgery Should Have        74
   Mental Health Screenings
   *Newsmax.com*

Periodical Bibliography                               79

# Chapter 3: Why Do People Have Cosmetic Surgery?

Chapter Preface     **81**

1. Most People Do Not Have Cosmetic Surgery for Vanity     **83**
   *Loren Eskenazi*

2. The Social Pressure to Have Cosmetic Surgery Has Increased     **93**
   *Karen Donley-Hayes*

3. Cosmetic Surgery Can Improve Self-Esteem     **99**
   *Rick Nauert*

4. Cosmetic Surgery May Not Improve Self-Esteem     **104**
   *Melissa Dittmann*

5. People Have Cosmetic Surgery to Appear Ageless     **113**
   *Amy Larocca*

6. People Who Have Cosmetic Surgery Want to Look Good for Their Age     **121**
   *Wendy Lewis*

7. People Have Cosmetic Surgery to Make More Money     **128**
   *Liz Wolgemuth*

Periodical Bibliography     **133**

# Chapter 4: What Is the Future of Cosmetic Surgery?

Chapter Preface     **135**

1. Cosmetic Surgery Should Be Taxed     **137**
   *Part I: Jessica Dweck, Part II: Claudia Deutsch*

2. Cosmetic Surgery Should Not Be Taxed     **141**
   *Haideh Hirmand*

3. More Men Get Cosmetic Surgery     **147**
   *Leah Hardy*

4. Stem Cells Will Improve Cosmetic Surgery     **152**
    *Richard Ellenbogen, as told to Connie Jennings*

Periodical Bibliography     **160**

For Further Discussion     **161**

Organizations to Contact     **163**

Bibliography of Books     **168**

Index     **171**

# Why Consider Opposing Viewpoints?

> *"The only way in which a human being can make some approach to knowing the whole of a subject is by hearing what can be said about it by persons of every variety of opinion and studying all modes in which it can be looked at by every character of mind. No wise man ever acquired his wisdom in any mode but this."*
>
> *John Stuart Mill*

In our media-intensive culture it is not difficult to find differing opinions. Thousands of newspapers and magazines and dozens of radio and television talk shows resound with differing points of view. The difficulty lies in deciding which opinion to agree with and which "experts" seem the most credible. The more inundated we become with differing opinions and claims, the more essential it is to hone critical reading and thinking skills to evaluate these ideas. Opposing Viewpoints books address this problem directly by presenting stimulating debates that can be used to enhance and teach these skills. The varied opinions contained in each book examine many different aspects of a single issue. While examining these conveniently edited opposing views, readers can develop critical thinking skills such as the ability to compare and contrast authors' credibility, facts, argumentation styles, use of persuasive techniques, and other stylistic tools. In short, the Opposing Viewpoints Series is an ideal way to attain the higher-level thinking and reading skills so essential in a culture of diverse and contradictory opinions.

In addition to providing a tool for critical thinking, Opposing Viewpoints books challenge readers to question their own strongly held opinions and assumptions. Most people form their opinions on the basis of upbringing, peer pressure, and personal, cultural, or professional bias. By reading carefully balanced opposing views, readers must directly confront new ideas as well as the opinions of those with whom they disagree. This is not to simplistically argue that everyone who reads opposing views will—or should—change his or her opinion. Instead, the series enhances readers' understanding of their own views by encouraging confrontation with opposing ideas. Careful examination of others' views can lead to the readers' understanding of the logical inconsistencies in their own opinions, perspective on why they hold an opinion, and the consideration of the possibility that their opinion requires further evaluation.

## Evaluating Other Opinions

To ensure that this type of examination occurs, Opposing Viewpoints books present all types of opinions. Prominent spokespeople on different sides of each issue as well as well-known professionals from many disciplines challenge the reader. An additional goal of the series is to provide a forum for other, less known, or even unpopular viewpoints. The opinion of an ordinary person who has had to make the decision to cut off life support from a terminally ill relative, for example, may be just as valuable and provide just as much insight as a medical ethicist's professional opinion. The editors have two additional purposes in including these less known views. One, the editors encourage readers to respect others' opinions—even when not enhanced by professional credibility. It is only by reading or listening to and objectively evaluating others' ideas that one can determine whether they are worthy of consideration. Two, the inclusion of such viewpoints encourages the important critical thinking skill of objectively evaluating an author's credentials and bias. This evaluation will illuminate an author's reasons for taking a particular stance on an issue and will aid in readers' evaluation of the author's ideas.

It is our hope that these books will give readers a deeper understanding of the issues debated and an appreciation of the complexity of even seemingly simple issues when good and honest people disagree. This awareness is particularly important in a democratic society such as ours in which people enter into public debate to determine the common good. Those with whom one disagrees should not be regarded as enemies but rather as people whose views deserve careful examination and may shed light on one's own.

Thomas Jefferson once said that "difference of opinion leads to inquiry, and inquiry to truth." Jefferson, a broadly educated man, argued that "if a nation expects to be ignorant and free . . . it expects what never was and never will be." As individuals and as a nation, it is imperative that we consider the opinions of others and examine them with skill and discernment. The Opposing Viewpoints Series is intended to help readers achieve this goal.

*David L. Bender and Bruno Leone,*
*Founders*

# Introduction

*"But as this wrinkle cure has continued to shoot up in popularity (it's the No. 1 non-surgical cosmetic treatment in the country), a Botox backlash is also brewing."*

—Diane Mapes, MSNBC.com,
October 22, 2007

In 2006, Botox reached more than $1 billion in sales, half of which was generated by the pursuit of Americans to smooth their frown lines, foreheads, and crow's-feet. How does it work? Botox is injected into wrinkle-causing muscles—binding to nerve endings and halting signals—and freezes them temporarily for a smoother appearance that lasts for several months. "Friends, family, and coworkers are eagerly talking to other people about their experiences with Botox," writes Deborah Mitchell in *The Botox Miracle*. "The stigma appears to be quickly fading as cosmetic rejuvenation becomes more and more acceptable."

Botox is the trade name for botulinum toxin type A, which is linked to botulism, a form of food poisoning. From 1817 to 1822, botulism was first studied by German scientist Justinus Kerner after several people died from consuming spoiled sausage. He was able to determine how botulism causes eyelids to droop, weakness of the muscles, and, in fatal cases, paralysis and respiratory failure. Recognizing the neurotoxin's deadliness, the United States adopted it as part of its biological weapons research during World War II, and the research evolved to medical applications after the war ended. In the 1960s, eye doctor Alan B. Scott pioneered the use of botulinum toxin type A to treat strabismus (crossed eyes) and blepharospasm (eyelid spasms). But it was another eye doctor,

Jean Carruthers, who found that the patients she treated with Botox had diminished facial lines, and she published a 1992 study on the findings with her husband, a dermatologist. It quickly gained widespread cosmetic use—resulting in a botulinum toxin type A shortage in 1997—and in 2002 Botox was approved by the Food and Drug Administration (FDA) for reducing frown lines.

Botox has been hailed as a revolutionary treatment for wrinkles, offering the benefits of cosmetic surgery without the invasive nipping and tucking. "The problem before was, we couldn't avoid gravity and sagging," states Jean-Louis Sebagh, a dermatologist based in London, England, in a November 2008 article in *People* magazine. "Now you really can. Botox is a preventative tool." For millions of patients, from celebrities to homemakers, it is part of their beauty routine, costing between $350 to $500 an injection. "To me, Botox is no more unusual than toothpaste," explains Simon Cowell, the British judge on *American Idol*, in the *People* article. "It works; you do it once a year." An online commentator at Wrinkles.org swears by the treatment, insisting that Botox is a career booster: "I shudder to think what I would look like without it, probably tired and angry. I truly believe that getting Botox regularly has helped me get promotions even."

Nonetheless, Botox and its effects are under skepticism. Some question its safety, as it is one of the most powerful poisons in existence. "In this atmosphere of Botox parties, where champagne-sipping socialites are injected with botulinum toxin, it is easy to forget that its very long-term effects are still unknown," contends V. Peter Misra, a British neurophysiologist, in an article in the *British Medical Journal*. Others cite the potential side effects, which include the unintentional spreading of the neurotoxin into other muscles, weakening them. And then there is the unexpected impact on entertainment— critics of Botox allege that it limits the abilities of some Hollywood actors to show emotion. "An ocean of Botox and collagen has been jabbed into the most famous faces on earth—leaving the audience feeling disconnected without knowing why," argues Johann Hari, a writer for the *Independent*. "Alfred Hitchcock once said, 'The greatest special effect is a close-up of the human face.' Botox has stripped this effect from the movies—and left our films frozen."

As relatively recent as the FDA's approval of cosmetic Botox was (it does not officially cover uses beyond reducing frown lines), it has strong competitors. Dysport, which works similarly to its predecessor, is cheaper by 20 percent. Other injectables, such as Juvéderm and Restylane, are gaining ground as weapons against lines and wrinkles. Furthermore, patients who desire more dramatic results will elect more invasive procedures including cosmetic surgery. *Opposing Viewpoints: Cosmetic Surgery* investigates what happens under the knife and afterward in the following chapters: Is Cosmetic Surgery Safe? Who Should Have Cosmetic Surgery? Why Do People Have Cosmetic Surgery? What Is the Future of Cosmetic Surgery? The group of authors in this volume offers a diverse range of expertise and insights on this billion-dollar industry.

OPPOSING
VIEWPOINTS®
SERIES

# CHAPTER 1

# Is Cosmetic Surgery Safe?

# Chapter Preface

In October 2009, California governor Arnold Schwarzenegger signed the Donda West Law, which requires a cosmetic surgery patient to first undergo a physical examination, disclose his or her medical history, and obtain written medical clearance. It is named after the late mother of rapper Kanye West; Donda West died in 2007 from complications she experienced the day after receiving liposuction and breast reduction. The Los Angeles County coroner concluded that Donda died from "multiple post-operative factors"[1] and coronary heart disease. "Sometimes patients may think they are well enough for cosmetic surgery, but in reality are not,"[2] stated assemblywoman Wilmer Amina Carter, a sponsor of the Donda West Law. "This bill will potentially save lives."

Adding a twist to the tragedy, another surgeon, Andre Aboolian, came forward and said he previously declined to perform surgery on Donda West because he was worried about her condition and age leading to a heart attack and urged her to get checked by an internist. "If, for God's sake, the surgeon tells you it's too risky, don't find someone who will do it for you,"[3] maintains Richard D'Amico, former president of the American Society of Plastic Surgeons (ASPS).

Whether Donda had a physical examination, however, remains in disagreement. The surgeon who performed her surgeries, Jan Adams, claims that she did, but Donda's niece, Yolanda Anderson, insists that she did not. Furthermore, some physicians believe that the law will not make cosmetic surgery safer. James Wells, also a former president of ASPS, argues

1. TMZ, "Coroner: Donda Had a Heart Attack," January 10, 2008. www.tmz.com.

2. Gil Kaufman, "Arnold Schwarzenegger Signs Donda West Plastic Surgery Law," MTV .com, October 15, 2009. www.mtv.com.

3. Jordan Lite and Nancy Dillon, "Kanye West's Mom Dies After Cosmetic Surgery," *New York Daily News*, November 13, 2007. www.nydailynews.com.

that it "codifies what reputable physicians have already been doing for a long time; it'll never change the guys who want to be outlaws to do anything different. They're going to do what they want to do."[4] In the following chapter, the authors debate the safety of the kinds of elective surgeries Donda West chose to have and other cosmetic procedures.

4. Madison Park, "Donda West Law Won't Boost Patient Safety, Docs Say," CNN.com, January 29, 2010. www.cnn.com.

> "Cosmetic surgery itself actually carries
> very minimal risk if you put yourself
> in the hands of a qualified, certified,
> cosmetic surgery specialist."

# Cosmetic Surgery Is Safe

### California Health and Beauty

*In the following viewpoint, California Health and Beauty contends that cosmetic surgery is safe when performed by a properly certified and trained surgeon. According to California Health and Beauty, patients must follow several guidelines before consulting with a surgeon: thoroughly investigate for credentials and malpractice claims, complete a medical examination prior to surgery, and adhere to the doctor's orders to abstain from certain activities or drugs. California Health and Beauty is owned by American Health and Beauty, a marketing site designed for cosmetic surgeons and other medical professionals.*

As you read, consider the following questions:

1. According to California Health and Beauty, how did Donda West's death affect the public's view of cosmetic surgery?

2. Why should patients be skeptical of cosmetic surgeons in the media, as stated by California Health and Beauty?

California Health and Beauty, "Surgery Is Safe According to Plastic Surgeon," November 25, 2007. Reproduced by permission.

3. Why is feeling comfortable with a cosmetic surgeon an important consideration, according to the viewpoint?

The fallout from the recent death of rapper Kanye West's mother, Dr. Donda West, is causing a far-reaching backlash against cosmetic surgery. As early investigations attribute the tragedy to "complications from a cosmetic surgical procedure," initial public reaction is to avoid cosmetic procedures all together, deeming them "too risky."

However, qualified plastic and reconstructive surgeons are speaking out in an effort to educate the public about the real risk of plastic surgery. According to Dr. Darshan Shah, a Mayo Clinic–trained board certified surgeon, clinical educator in plastic surgery, and three-time winner of the prestigious "Best of Bakersfield" award for cosmetic procedures, "Cosmetic surgery itself actually carries very minimal risk if you put yourself in the hands of a qualified, certified cosmetic surgery specialist—someone who has trained and devoted [his or her] career to the field of plastic and reconstructive surgery. . . . The real risk lies not in the surgery itself, but in the misrepresentation and inexperience of certain surgeons."

Dr. Shah advises would-be patients that, "The most important thing is research. It is crucial that patients do their own research prior to even consulting with a surgeon." And while Dr. Shah himself has appeared on shows such as *Dr. Phil* and *Extreme Makeover*, he stresses that the public can not trust the media to research a doctor's qualifications. It has been uncovered that Dr. Jan Adams (the doctor involved in the Donda West incident) had been a frequent guest on the *Oprah Winfrey Show* as well as involved in his own makeover program, yet, in fact, is not board eligible or certified in plastic surgery, and, according to the Web site for the California Medical Board, has been sued numerous times for medical malpractice. "By no means does a TV appearance signify that

**Speed Bump**

Used with permission of Dave Coverly and the Cartoonist Group. License 2010-204.

a doctor is a qualified cosmetic surgeon ... anyone considering plastic surgery must do their own research into a surgeon's history and medical qualifications," warns Dr. Shah.

## Potentially Lifesaving Guidelines

But researching the doctor's training is not the only protective measure: In an effort to educate the public, Dr. Shah shares his list of potentially lifesaving guidelines for safe cosmetic surgery.

1. *Thoroughly investigate training and credentials*. Again, don't trust TV personalities to verify credentials: Visit Web sites like the Medical Board of California, the American Board of Plastic Surgery, or the American College of Surgeons. Make sure the doctor has specifically been trained in the field of plastic surgery; too often we find anesthesiologists, ob/gyns or even family practice doctor performing surgery which they are not qualified to do.

2. *Search for malpractice claims*. One of the best indicators of incompetence is malpractice claims or settlements. Chances are good that if a surgeon is practicing in an unethical manner, someone has complained—the Federation of State Medical Boards is a good resource for tracking disciplinary actions. Finally, do a quick Google or Yahoo search on both the name of the surgeon as well as the surgery center itself and see what comes up; check for any negative reports associated with either name.

3. *Meet the (wo)man*. While some may argue that you don't need to click on a personal level to have a safe surgical experience (and in fact Dr. Adams himself appears quite charming), feeling comfortable with your doctor is actually an important consideration. If you feel at ease, you are more likely to address your fears and ask the questions that will paint the fullest picture of the doctor's competencies. Furthermore, there are certain red flags to look for such as a doctor who seems to be persuading you to have a surgery or who actively pushes additional procedures. When meeting a potential surgeon, the vibe you should be getting from him is one of caution, no matter what the procedure.

4. *A medical exam is a must*. Any qualified surgeon will require all patients over 50, or any patients with medical

problems, to undergo a full medical evaluation prior to surgery . . . and will review the results personally. If your doctor discredits the need for a full workup or simply takes your word that you are "in good health," you need to find another doctor. And disappointing as it may be, if the results of your exam indicate you are not a good candidate for cosmetic surgery, heed the warning—"doctor shopping" until you find a surgeon who'll agree to perform the procedure is one of the most common causes of disaster.

5. *Follow the doctor's orders.* There are good reasons doctors give instructions prior to surgery; ignore them and you may be putting your life in peril. Whether it's quitting smoking or avoiding alcohol or aspirin, when it comes to preoperative orders, caution is king.

6. *Be honest with your surgeon.* This should go without saying, but it is extremely risky to withhold information about your medical history in an effort to get your doctor to approve a surgery. Even if you think it's irrelevant, be sure to disclose all medical conditions (past or present), prior surgeries, and medications or drug use— your doctor is bound by the laws of confidentiality, so disclose to avoid danger.

7. *Be honest with yourself.* While this is not so much a matter of safety as it is psychological health, the best way to assure a positive outcome is to be honest with yourself (and your doctor) regarding your expectations. Cosmetic surgery is not to be taken lightly; make sure you identify the reasons you desire a procedure, what you feel will change as a result, and that your goals regarding the surgery are realistic. For example, liposuction or breast enhancement may boost your confidence at the beach, but they will not address underlying depression or solve interpersonal issues.

*"When you sign up for surgery, you risk dying to look good."*

# Cosmetic Surgery Is Dangerous

*Jenny Kleeman*

*In the following viewpoint, Jenny Kleeman asserts that as cosmetic surgery becomes more popular and accessible, the risks of injury, illness, and death are underestimated. Changing cultural attitudes and makeover television shows have lessened the stigma of cosmetic procedures, but in reality, the author reiterates that tummy tucks, liposuctions, and breast augmentations are major surgeries. Nonetheless, she states that such procedures are perceived as quick fixes, despite being much more dangerous than dieting, counseling, and other forms of self-improvement. Kleeman is a British journalist and documentary filmmaker.*

1. In the author's opinion, what words are used to describe plastic surgery today?

2. Why are deaths related to cosmetic surgery unknown in the United Kingdom, according to Kleeman?

3. Why are people who have lost loved ones to cosmetic surgery complications unlikely to share their experiences, in Kleeman's view?

In the early evening of Friday July 20 [2007], Pauline Bainbridge had liposuction on her thighs. The procedure took less than an hour and she was delighted that it had gone so smoothly. By Saturday, she was out of the clinic and drinking tea on the sofa with her husband, Alan. The couple ate supper and watched a DVD until Pauline nodded off.

On Sunday, Pauline got out of bed and collapsed. Alan called an ambulance, but by the time it reached hospital, Pauline's heart had stopped. The casualty doctors treated her for a blood clot. They resuscitated her several times and gave her two blood transfusions. But less than 48 hours after surgery, Pauline was dead. She was 50.

"I didn't think cosmetic surgery could kill anyone," says Alan at their home in Poulton-le-Fylde, near Blackpool. "You hear about people with boob jobs having them done 20 times. I thought nothing could harm her except for the anaesthetic and that risk is remote if you are fit as a fiddle, like she was." He shakes his head. "It was an unbelievable shock. I still can't get my head around it."

Alan's disbelief is understandable. Over two decades or so, cosmetic surgery has gone from being the guilty secret of the rich and famous to something so everyday and acceptable that you can watch it most nights of the week on television— sometimes live, sometimes pre-recorded so the viewer can instantly compare before and after, sometimes overseen by presenters who frown on featured subjects who have let themselves go when surgical solutions are so readily available. Cosmetic surgery has lost its stigma and become something you get done in your lunch hour, like a leg wax or a haircut. It comes with its own new, euphemistic vocabulary: it's not surgery, it's a "boost"; you aren't being operated on, you are "getting something done".

Sometimes this language goes too far. This week [in December 2007], the Advertising Standards Authority [ASA] banned a poster campaign by the Harley Medical Group [HMG] that bore the slogan, "Gorgeous breasts just got easy with cosmetic surgery." HMG said they were surprised that anyone had complained about the advert, which featured a bikini-clad, flat-chested woman frowning for the "before" shot, and then grinning broadly with a bulging chest in the "after" picture. The ASA's ruling was unequivocal: "Because we understood that surgery always carried a risk to the patient, we concluded that, by promoting a surgical operation as 'easy', the approach was irresponsible and misleading."

## Never Easy or Risk Free

Surgery can never be easy or risk free—even when the patient can afford the very best care. Last month, the rapper Kanye West lost his mother, Donda, who apparently developed complications following a tummy tuck and breast reduction. Donda was 58, a former professor of English who had given up a 31-year tenured post to manage her son's business affairs. Stella Obasanjo, the first lady of Nigeria, died in 2005, aged 59, after a tummy tuck in a Spanish clinic. James Brown's third wife, Adrienne, died in 1996, aged 47, following an undisclosed cosmetic procedure. In 2004, Olivia Goldsmith, author of the *First Wives Club*, suffered a fatal heart attack at 54 as she was being prepared for a chin tuck.

No one knows for sure how many people die as a result of cosmetic surgery every year in the UK [United Kingdom]. The [government-run] NHS [National Health Service] has data on patients admitted to NHS hospitals due to complications from cosmetic surgery—there were 126 last year—but the Department of Health says this is nowhere near the true number of patients with post-surgery problems because many will be treated privately. Neither the Department of Health nor the British Association of Aesthetic Plastic Surgeons (BAAPS) collects figures on fatalities from cosmetic procedures, and death certificates are unlikely to give the cause of death as an adverse reaction to surgery, anyway—it is more likely to be attributed to the immediate cause, such as heart attack, haemorrhage, infection, or blood clot. But one thing is certain: Every year in the UK people die from unnecessary procedures, leaving partners and children behind.

The Bainbridges had been told this at their original consultation with Pauline's surgeon. "He said there can always be complications with any operation, but he hadn't lost anyone yet," Alan remembers. "He'd done a couple of thousand operations. He was a proper cosmetic surgeon, the top man."

Pauline was married to a man she had met when she was 17, and together they built a successful textile printing business. Alan describes her as the "hub" of their large extended family, the sort of person who would think nothing of inviting 30 people over for a barbecue if it looked as if it was going to be a warm afternoon. "She did everything on the house," Alan smiles. "She could have been an interior designer. That's what she was like—everything had to be perfect. She was a perfectionist."

She had fretted over the size of her thighs for years. "She was very slim on top, but always what I would call hippy—that was just the way she was built. All she ever wanted was to wear nice trouser suits or jeans and look a bit better. When Pauline turned 50, we had built the business up, we had built the house up, we had built the family up, and everyone was getting a bit older, so she said, 'Right, I'm going to do something for me for once—I'm going to have it done.'

"I was a typical man. I said, 'What are you wasting money for?'" Alan says. But a few weeks later, Pauline rang Alan at his office and told him she was having a consultation with a cosmetic surgeon, and suggested he should come and join them. The surgeon told her she would never have "Miss World legs", but he would be able to trim them a bit, so that she would feel better. Pauline agreed on the spot and signed up for lipo-suction in three weeks time, at a cost of more than £3,000. It all sounded very simple, and she reckoned she would be fully recovered in time for a break in Florida that they had booked for October.

The trip to Florida went ahead—but without Pauline. Instead, a grieving Alan took their two sons. It was a good opportunity for them to get away from the house, the cards and the flowers, which are still arriving, four months after Pauline's death.

Pauline hadn't told anyone else that she was having lipo-suction. She didn't want anyone to worry about it, Alan says, and wanted to surprise everyone with her new thighs. So when Alan arrived at the hospital on the day his wife collapsed, and was told that she was in a critical condition, he had to break the news to her family that not only was Pauline dying, but she was dying because of something that she had chosen to do.

Pauline's sisters came to the hospital, along with her 23-year-old son, Danny. Her elder son, Paul, 26, was on holiday in Cuba and Alan finally managed to contact him while his mother was being resuscitated. "I said, 'You've got to get yourself home, right now. Your mum's seriously ill in hospital,'" Alan remembers. "He started screaming and crying down the phone at me. It was awful. I never want to go through that again. What the hell do you do? Do you tell him? Do you wait until he gets home?

"Some people were angry when they found out she'd had the surgery. One of her sisters said, 'Stupid, stupid woman!' But nobody blamed me for letting her have it done, because they knew she wanted it, and she was a very strong person."

When the consultant came to break the news that Pauline had died, he was met with a room full of her extended family. "He looked at all our faces—we were so distraught—and he just said, 'I'm sorry'. You can imagine what that room was like.

And my son was there to see it too." Alan falters. "We came out with nothing, and we just . . . went home."

Alan doesn't hold anyone responsible for what happened to his wife and doubts the results of the forthcoming coroner's report will make any difference to the way he feels now. "I know in my mind that I have to carry on because I've got two lads, I've got a house, I've got a business, and people rely on me," he says. "But after 33 years together, it's just horrendous.

"I wouldn't recommend anyone having cosmetic surgery done ever, ever. I don't think you should have an operation anyway, unless you really need one."

## By No Means Extraordinary

Pauline's story is shocking, but by no means extraordinary. Alexandra Mills was only 20 when she died after a procedure on her jaw two years ago. She had attended performing arts college near her home in Cirencester, and dreamed of becoming an actress. She was taking a gap year, working as a waitress to save up money for drama school, when she went in for the surgery.

"When she was little, she was teased at school because of her chin, so she didn't want to let it stand in the way of her career. That's why she had the operation," her mother, Jane, said after the inquest into Alexandra's death last year.

The eight-hour operation to break and reset Alexandra's jaw was a routine procedure and part of a long-term plan to correct her jawline. Surgeons initially hailed it as a success, but after the operation, a tube to monitor her blood pressure shifted, and pierced her heart. The potassium she was given to aid recovery then leaked into her heart and triggered a massive heart attack. This freak set of post-surgery complications left her with extensive brain damage and Alexandra died four days afterwards. "Everyone who knew her loved her and thought she was wonderful. She was full of life and spirit," says Jane. "We don't cry as much now, but it's still terribly difficult."

Neither Pauline's nor Alexandra's surgeons were to blame—surgery carries a risk and both patients were fully informed. But even in cases where relatives have successfully sued, the loss of a healthy loved one during routine surgery is no less bewildering. Lorraine Batt left three children behind when she died in 1999, aged 36, following a £5,500 tummy tuck. Once again, the operation seemed to have been a success, but the following day Lorraine complained of headache and nausea. She fell into a coma and died from swelling of the brain three days after surgery.

Her husband, David, has described Lorraine as someone who "loved clothes and always wanted to look her best". She wanted to lose the weight she had gained after having children, and to correct loose skin and scarring on her stomach left by a caesarean section. But according to her father, Eddie Fisher, Lorraine didn't have much weight to lose. "She weighed just nine-and-a-half stone and was a smashing girl."

David won £260,000 compensation in 2004 after an inquest heard evidence that Lorraine should never have been allowed to have the procedure in the first place because she had already been diagnosed with an underactive thyroid. He gave up his job as a builder in Wickford, Essex, to look after their daughter, Kayla, who was only seven when she lost her mother. "This is the end of a terrible episode for my family," he said after the court ruling. "The money doesn't ease the pain. The figure is ridiculous and it is not what I hoped for. But I think I would have been disappointed with any amount."

## Surgery of Choice

Dr Steven Chan, who conducted the inquest, did not mince his words. "I have no doubt of the determination of the deceased when she agreed to go through with major surgery," he said, "but the point must be made that all surgery could result in complications with devastating effects. There is no safe surgery."

Few of those who have been bereaved by cosmetic surgery are prepared to speak at length about their experiences. Their loved ones had put themselves at risk voluntarily—and often needlessly—for the sake of looking better. In a way, this robs them of the dignity in death that others who have died suddenly can expect, and makes it especially painful for relatives to go over what happened to them.

Equally, those who have come close to death after cosmetic surgery may feel ashamed of the recklessness of their decision to have it done. Denise Hendry, who is married to the former Scottish football captain, Colin Hendry, was back in hospital last month, five years after botched liposuction left her in a coma for five weeks.

"I had done all this out of vanity and put my family through all that worry. I just wanted a quick fix after having four babies," she said after the surgery. "I felt so bad when I thought Colin could have lost his wife, my children would have lost their mother, my mum and dad lost a daughter and my sister would have lost her sister. I felt overwhelming guilt at how stupid I had been."

Douglas McGeorge, consultant plastic surgeon and president of BAAPS, says is it "incredibly unusual" for a patient to die from cosmetic surgery, and dismisses the idea that cosmetic procedures are unnecessary risks. "These people have got a problem, in the main. We have things that can be done to improve their problems. At the end of the day, aesthetic surgery is done for improving quality of life.

"It is, by definition, surgery of choice, and you don't do it on people who run significant risks. We're not operating on obese people, we are not operating on people who have cancer," he says. "In reality, it's probably more dangerous driving to hospital for most of these individuals."

But these operations are certainly riskier than having counselling, wearing control pants, buying a padded bra or going on a diet. As cosmetic surgery becomes an increasingly normal part of our culture, we are in danger of forgetting just what makes it different from conventional beauty treatments: When you sign up for surgery, you risk dying to look good.

> *"Through word of mouth and the Internet, patients hook up with doctors overseas, discuss prices and procedures, and make appointments."*

# Cosmetic Surgery Tourism Is Safe

## John Otis

*In the following viewpoint, John Otis claims that a growing number of foreigners are traveling to South America for cosmetic surgery at a fraction of the cost. He says that Americans and Europeans head to Colombia, Argentina, and Brazil to connect with highly skilled surgeons, receive personalized medical care, and see the world. Patients, however, are recommended to avoid clinics with slashed prices and unqualified doctors, as anyone with a medical degree can practice cosmetic surgery legally in some regions, Otis maintains. Based in Bogotá, Colombia, the author is a correspondent for GlobalPost and served as the South American bureau chief for the* Houston Chronicle.

As you read, consider the following questions:

1. How did Colombia attract foreigners seeking cosmetic surgery, as stated by Otis?

John Otis, "Sun, Surf, and Scalpels," *Houston Chronicle*, December 2, 2007. p. 25. Copyright © 2007 Houston Chronicle Publishing Company Division. Republished with permission of Houston Chronicle, conveyed through CopyrightClearance Center, Inc.

2. What is the American Society of Plastic Surgeons' position on cosmetic surgery tourism?

3. What did Monica Yesquen discuss with her surgeon before her surgery, as described in the viewpoint?

Lacking $40,000 for cosmetic surgery in the United States, New York resident Monica Yesquen opted to overhaul her body in Colombia.

During a six-hour operation, a Colombian plastic surgeon lifted Yesquen's face, straightened her chin, lipo-sucked her abdomen and removed a five-pound slab of skin and fat from her belly. The total cost: $10,000.

Yesquen is one of a growing number of foreigners flocking to Colombia and other Latin American nations for nose jobs, breast implants and other nips and tucks to enhance their sagging, middle-aged bodies.

Hundreds of clinics have sprung up across the region featuring top-notch surgeons and low prices, a key combination since American health insurance plans rarely cover plastic surgery.

Through word of mouth and the Internet, patients hook up with doctors overseas, discuss prices and procedures, and make appointments. Travel agencies specializing in medical tourism offer all-inclusive vacation/surgical packages.

"I came to Colombia because it's cheaper than Spain," said Aurora Baquero, a homemaker from Madrid who flew to the Colombian city of Cali for a laundry list of cosmetic enhancements. "They've done everything to me: nose job, eyelids, face, bust, thighs. My mother won't recognize me anymore."

## Affordable Destination

Bogota is home to 60 clinics that specialize in plastic surgery. Once known for their cocaine cartels, Cali and Medellin are now meccas for tummy tucks and liposuction.

Clinics in these cities offer nose jobs for $2,000 and breast augmentations for $2,500, procedures that would cost about $6,500 and $8,500, respectively, in the United States.

Adding to Colombia's allure is its fascination with beauty pageants, which usually feature enhanced contestants, and the fact that soccer legend Diego Maradona, who was desperate to lose weight, traveled here in 2005 for gastric bypass surgery. All told, tourist officials estimate that more than 30,000 foreigners visit Colombia annually for cosmetic surgery.

"I operate on six to eight foreigners per month," said Celso Bohorquez, a physician and spokesman for the Colombian Society of Plastic Surgery, who performed the tummy tuck and face lift on Yesquen. Besides better-looking bodies, he added, "they get to travel and get to know the world."

The globalization of medical treatment has been a boon for health providers in other Latin American nations. Although it's difficult for foreign surgeons to practice in the U.S. and Europe, it's relatively easy for patients to travel to Latin America.

In Argentina, the 2002 economic crisis that collapsed the currency made plastic surgery more affordable to tourists and led to an influx. In Brazil, officials estimate that about 50,000 tourists annually arrive for medical treatment, including cosmetic surgery.

Once in country, patients often find highly skilled plastic surgeons.

## Choose Doctors Carefully

In Rio, the Brazilian capital for cosmetic surgery, procedures cost 30 percent to 50 percent less than in the United States. But Luis Carlos Celi Garcia, the past president of the Brazilian Plastic Surgeon's Association, said price is only one of the attractions.

"Money is not the only issue. If the quality was bad, people wouldn't come back," he said. Alluding to the gorgeous seafront neighborhoods of Copacabana and Ipanema, he added:

## Cosmetic Surgery's Most Popular Destinations

| Country | Savings | Travel Time | English |
|---|---|---|---|
| Brazil | ** | ** | * |
| Costa Rica | ** | *** | ** |
| Malaysia | *** | * | *** |
| Singapore | ** | * | *** |
| Thailand | ** | * | ** |

**Savings**
***Highest savings
**Great savings
*Good savings

**Travel time (flight only from Los Angeles)**
***Under 10 hours
**10–20 hours
*20+ hours

**English**
***Widely spoken
**Spoken only in metropolitan areas
*Not widely spoken

TAKEN FROM: Patrick W. Marsek, Frances Sharpe, *The Complete Idiot's Guide to Medical Tourism*. New York: Alpha Books, 2009.

"They come to spend time on the beach and then they get their operations."

But patients are advised to choose their doctors carefully.

In Colombia, anyone with a medical degree can legally perform plastic surgery even if they have never specialized in the practice. Garage-like clinics have sprung up in Bogota and Cali, where unqualified doctors offer rock-bottom prices.

"We've had four or five cases where people come to us to help them correct bad plastic surgery," said Diana Richardson of Turismedic, a Bogota-based travel agency that brings foreigners here for cosmetic surgery. After a botched operation, she added, "one woman complained that her breasts hung down to her belly button."

## Connecting with a Patient

The American Society of Plastic Surgeons cautions that patients may take unnecessary risks when choosing cosmetic surgery vacations by inadvertently selecting unqualified physicians. The organization also warns that vacations and major surgery often don't mix.

"To properly heal and reduce the possibility of complications, patients should not sunbathe, drink alcohol, swim, snorkel, parasail or exercise after surgery," the society said in a briefing paper on cosmetic surgery tourism. But Yesquen, the patient from New York, says the U.S. medical system has its own problems. She described American doctors as cold, impersonal and expensive.

"They don't care about you once the operation is over," said Yesquen, a 46-year-old Chilean who moved to New York 15 years ago. "They just collect your money."

Over the years, Yesquen had put on weight and was unable to stick to diets or exercise. She couldn't afford plastic surgery in the United States, so she considered Colombia. Besides low prices, cosmetic surgery packages here include private nurses, post-operation therapy and follow-up consultations with the doctors.

Through the Turismedic agency, Yesquen got in touch with Bohorquez. They e-mailed messages and photos back and forth and settled on a handful of procedures that could be performed during one marathon operation. Joking with Dr. Bohorquez as he wheeled her into the operating room, Yesquen smiled and said: "I hope everything works out and that I'll also look beautiful."

## 'I Made the Best Decision'

The surgery itself was long, tedious and gory.

During the tummy tuck, Dr. Bohorquez used metal spatulas, scalpels and laser cutters to slice away a half-moon-shaped wedge of Yesquen's stomach that nurses later weighed on a scale for newborn babies. Liposuction tubes clogged up with a liquid mix of red blood and yellow fat.

"It's grotesque," Bohorquez admitted from behind his face mask.

Yet the end result was impressive. A week after surgery, Yesquen sported black-and-blue eyes and bandages on her chin, but she looked years younger.

"My stomach is flat. I feel so good," said Yesquen, as she toured Bogota's colonial downtown with her own private tour guide provided by Turismedic. "I made the best decision coming to this country."

> "As the lipotourism . . . grows, some American doctors are concerned about the quality of care patients who go there receive."

# Cosmetic Surgery Tourism Is Dangerous

## Victoria Corderi

*In the following viewpoint, Victoria Corderi asserts that patients lured to foreign countries with the promise of cut-rate cosmetic surgery place their bodies and lives at risk. Corderi states that tourists who had traveled to the Dominican Republic for bargain-priced liposuction, tummy tucks, and breast implants have suffered life-threatening injuries and conditions without adequate medical care. Even with a suspended license and an alarming track record, the doctor responsible for some of these extreme makeover disasters continued to operate his practice, she adds. Corderi is an award-winning journalist and correspondent for NBC News.*

As you read, consider the following questions:

1. As stated in the viewpoint, why did New York City's Health Department issue a warning about cosmetic surgery in the Dominican Republic?

Victoria Corderi, "Plastic Surgery Tourism?" *Dateline NBC*, March 18, 2005. Reproduced by permission.

2. How did Corderi test Edgar Contreras's practice?

3. According to Corderi, what is Contreras's explanation for pressure on Dominican surgeons?

In today's nip-and-tuck world, it seems more and more people long for extreme makeovers. For most, though, it's a costly fantasy that's way out of reach. But not for these women. They thought they'd found a way to make it happen.

Maria Morel, a mother of three from Newark, N.J., had been dropping hints about plastic surgery to her family for a long time.

Sonia Wilmoth, a 37-year-old secretary and mother from Boston, says she was so ashamed of her flabby belly and stretch marks she wouldn't even undress in front of her husband. Sonia says she was such an avid fan of makeover shows, she even called the plastic surgeons on television.

And these two best friends also had the same wish. Allyn Segura, a single mother living in Miami, and Yvonne Tamayo, an immigration consultant in New York, talked about plastic surgery on the phone constantly.

So how did the women find a way to make their surgical dreams come true on a budget? All they had to do was become part of the multi-million-dollar lipotourism trade, a business built around two ideas: foreign doctors who offer cut-rate surgery and Americans who are willing to go overseas to go under the knife.

Who wouldn't be tempted by the idea of sun, fun and surgery at unbeatable prices? Consider this: A tummy tuck in the United States would set you back at least $6,000, but in Costa Rica it's only $2,000. A facelift in the U.S. costs up to $9,000. In Malaysia it costs a third of that. And a breast augmentation in the U.S. costs $7,000, but in the Dominican Republic, only $2,000.

In fact, the Dominican Republic is fast becoming the Caribbean mecca of lipotourism. Eighty percent of the plastic surgery patients there come from abroad, lured by low prices and a seductive climate. But as the lipotourism in the Dominican Republic grows, some American doctors are concerned about the quality of care patients who go there receive. And, as we found, choosing one questionable doctor can lead to tragic consequences.

You can find ads for clinics in the Dominican Republic on Web sites, but much of the business is drummed up by word of mouth in an unusual setting that is anything but clinical—mom-and-pop beauty salons.

*Dateline* went to one in Manhattan with our hidden cameras last November. There were dozens of women jammed in the salon, many of them waiting for an appointment. And it wasn't just any appointment. They were prepared to wait for hours, if they had to. They had paid the manager of the salon $15 to meet a plastic surgeon who was pitching his clinic in the Dominican Republic.

And business is good. The salon owner tells us about the doctor's busy schedule. She was a walking, talking advertisement for the doctor's work.

While they waited to meet him, many of the women were just as open to talking about the surgery they want. There was lots of laughter and anticipation among the women, but what we didn't hear was anyone talking about what could go wrong.

Sonia, the secretary from Boston also got a recommendation for a plastic surgeon from her hairdresser.

*Sonia*: "She goes, 'Oh listen, I'll give you the guy that does me.' I said what do you mean? 'You know my plastic surgeon in the Dominican Republic.'"

Sonia couldn't believe what the doctor told her over the phone.

*Sonia*: "He said he would do the tummy tuck, the lipo in the back, and breast uplift all for $3,000. American dollars."

What a deal, her very own extreme, and extremely cheap makeover. Procedures that would have cost upwards of $15,000 in the United States would be 80 percent cheaper in the Dominican Republic. She was in and within weeks was on a plane to get her dream surgery. There was no research, it was based totally on the word of the hairdresser. Sonia says word of mouth was enough, along with the price tag.

Allyn and Yvonne, the two best friends, were also pretty confident that nothing bad would happen to them when they set out for the Dominican Republic last July. Allyn, a former nurse, had a list of questions to ask three doctors, who had been recommended by friends, family and of course, people at the beauty salon.

The friends decided on the last surgeon they interviewed. They say he answered all their questions and seemed very concerned. They say he accepted credit cards. And they were wowed by his prices—$2,500 apiece for a tummy tuck and extensive liposuction, surgery which would have cost them upwards of $15,000 in the United States.

Meanwhile Maria Morel, the mother of three from New Jersey, was planning to go ahead with her surgery, too, and she was going to make it a top-secret operation. She wanted to surprise her family with her new body.

Last November, according to her family, Maria said she was going on a business trip to the Dominican Republic. When she got there, she immediately checked into a clinic for a tummy tuck and liposuction. Her plan didn't quite unfold the way she'd imagined. Instead of surprise, her family is now feeling stunned.

Lipotourism is booming in the Dominican Republic. More than 1,000 Americans have surgery there every year. And while many have success, others find that their bargain basement surgery may come with hidden, even life-threatening costs.

Dr. Scott Spear is president of the American Society of Plastic Surgeons.

*Dr. Scott Spear*: "It's really scary to me that someone would get on an airplane and fly to a foreign country where there's no resort to help if there's a problem."

Last May, Sonia from Boston flew to a clinic in the Dominican Republic after being promised a great deal. She says her problems began even before the surgery was over. She says she woke up twice during the surgery.

*Sonia*: "During the surgery. I literally felt their hands inside my stomach."

When Sonia came to she says she was shaking uncontrollably and numb. She realized she was in trouble. An infection began destroying the skin around her incision. She turned to plastic surgeon Dr. Loren Borud for help. Borud says the Dominican doctor performed more surgery than Sonia's body could handle.

*Dr. Loren Borud*: "Anyone who does that operation should know those technical points. This should never happen. Should never happen."

Less than three months later, lipotourists and best friends Allyn and Yvonne checked into a Dominican plastic surgery clinic for their surgical overhaul. Were they making the right decision? That question was soon answered for both women.

Allyn wound up in a hospital in Miami, battling a massive infection. It turns out Allyn's surgeon had left her belly button floating inside her stomach instead of reattaching it. It deteriorated, causing an infection.

Meanwhile, her friend Yvonne was admitted to a hospital in New York City with a rare bacteria in her blood.

*Dr. Tornambe*: "The infection that she had when she came back from her initial surgery could have killed her."

They weren't the only lipotourists who returned to the United States with life-threatening complications. Last year U.S. health officials identified an unusual and virulent bacteria in 16 women who'd had plastic surgery in the Dominican Republic. The Centers for Disease Control [and Prevention] warned doctors all over the country to be on the lookout. And that prompted New York City's Health Department to take a dramatic step, issuing a warning for people not to travel to the Dominican Republic for cosmetic surgery.

But not everyone heard or listened to that warning. Maria Morel flew from New Jersey to the Dominican Republic last November and checked into a clinic for her long-awaited surgery. But when Maria called her husband from a recovery room at the clinic he said something seemed seriously wrong with her breathing.

Her family says Maria asked to see a lung specialist. Instead they say she got an oxygen tank. Six days later, Maria was dead.

Trabys, her eldest daughter, still can't make sense of it and Jose, her husband of 28 years is haunted by what was done to his wife. Within two weeks of Maria's death, the Morel family marched to the prosecutor's office in Santo Domingo and demanded the doctor be investigated.

The doctor is Edgar Contreras, and he's the same doctor who operated on Sonia from Boston, Allyn from Miami and Yvonne from New York. He's a celebrity in the Dominican Republic, as famous for his work on beauty queens as he is for his medical record. It turns out Maria Morel was not the first person to die after visiting his clinic.

In 1998 one of his patients, a woman from Puerto Rico died from multiple complications after surgery. Six months later, another woman died of a heart attack brought on by the strain of too much surgery.

The cases caused a media frenzy, and in 1999 Dr. Contreras was charged with two counts or involuntary homicide even though he said the women died of natural causes. The cases have yet to come to trial and the doors of his clinic have stayed open for business to unsuspecting patients like Maria Morel, Allyn, Sonia and Yvonne.

We wanted to find out more about Dr. Contreras and the services he offers lipotourists, so we made an appointment.

We flew to the Dominican Republic, taking with us Dr. Loren Borud, Sonia Wilmoth's plastic surgeon. Borud says he's concerned about complications he is seeing from some surgery performed there.

*Dr. Borud*: "There's significant judgment problems and significant technical problems that are occurring there."

*Corderi*: "I can hear the plastic surgery society in the DR [Dominican Republic] saying, you know, of course American doctors are saying that because they're losing business."

*Dr. Borud*: "We're not having problems not having enough patients to operate on here in America. We're almost ethically bound to identify a problem that we think is really malpractice."

Borud accompanied me when I met with Dr. Contreras to give his professional impression of the appointment.

*Dr. Borud*: "He was perfectly willing to take the time and answer all of our questions."

What Contreras did not do, Borud said, was ask me about my medical history. As a test, I told him I was taking a drug that should have disqualified me as a patient. It thins the blood and may cause excessive bleeding during the surgery. Dr. Contreras said it didn't matter. I could do surgery the next day.

*Dr. Borud*: "If this were the only evaluation that would be quite negligent."

A few days later we took our cameras into the clinic after hours. This is the emergency room where Contreras told us patients who develop complications are treated. It's a tiny L-shaped room with no apparent medical equipment.

And to get there a critically ill patient would have to sit or stand in this narrow elevator, too small to accommodate a gurney.

During our investigation we met former patients from the United States who told us they were repulsed by conditions at the clinic. One woman says she was prescribed a skin cream for her scars that is not even intended for humans.

Perhaps most surprising is that Dr. Contreras is practicing at all. According to a 1999 court order obtained by *Dateline NBC*, Contreras's license in the Dominican Republic is suspended. We took the document to Roxana Reyes, an attorney at the prosecutor's office.

*Corderi*: "That shows you according to the law he should not be practicing medicine."

*Roxana Reyes*: "Yes that's it."

*Corderi*: "So why is he practicing medicine?"

*Reyes*: "The problem is we don't have enough people to watch the thing."

*Corderi*: "Isn't it just a matter of driving to the clinic, closing the doors and putting a lock on it? He seems to be laughing at the law."

*Reyes*: "If he continues practicing without permission, he is violating the law."

We wanted to talk to Dr. Contreras but he turned down our repeated requests for an interview. Instead, he told Dominican journalists *Dateline NBC* was pressuring the prosecutor's office on behalf of American plastic surgeons who were unhappy about losing business to the Dominican Republic. Contreras also told reporters that Maria Morel died from natural causes.

Days later, a judge decided Contreras should be jailed until he stands trial for involuntary homicide for the death of Maria Morel. He was taken into custody until his family posted bail.

Even though American surgeons we spoke with said Dr. Contreras may be an extreme example, they say it's important for people to research any surgeon they are considering, both here and abroad.

*Dr. Scott Spear:* "You know one difference between us and automobiles—you can throw the car away and buy a new one. But you're stuck with your body. You should make decisions about your body very carefully."

But that advice comes too late for the Morel family particularly three-year-old Jose who is still waiting for his mother to come home.

*Trabys:* "It hurts every time he asks me like where's Mommy and I have to tell him she's dead. I know how much he misses his mother."

# Periodical Bibliography

*The following articles have been selected to supplement the diverse views presented in this chapter.*

Jessica Bernstein-Wax "Mexican Doctor Charged with Posing as Plastic Surgeon, Botching Dozens of Operations," *Associated Press*, December 28, 2007.

Elizabeth Cohen "What Really Killed the Beauty Queen?" CNN.com, December 10, 2009. www.cnn.com.

Maura Corrigan "Stay Safe at the Med Spa," *Self*, August 2009.

Vivian Diller "Cosmetics Drugs Gone Too Far: Is Anything Still Real?" *Psychology Today*, July 14, 2010.

Charis Atlas Heelan "Cosmetic Surgery Tourism: A Tummy Tuck in Thailand, a Breast Augmentation in Brazil," Frommers.com, September 6, 2005. www.frommers.com.

Dan Lett "The Search for Integrity in the Cosmetic Surgery Market," *Canadian Medical Association Journal*, January 29, 2008.

*Medical News Today* "Cosmetic Surgery Patients at More Risk than Ever," November 16, 2009.

January W. Payne "Autopsy of Kanye West's Mother Underscores Surgery Risks," *U.S. News & World Report*, January 17, 2008.

Dominic Phillips "Is Plastic Surgery Dangerous?" *Sunday Times* (London), December 13, 2009.

Rich Smith "Patient Satisfaction Is Key," *Plastic Surgery Practice*, January 2009.

Andrew D. Swain "The Hidden Dangers of 'Medical' Spas," *Trial*, May 1, 2009.

CHAPTER 2

# Who Should Have Cosmetic Surgery?

# Chapter Preface

For her fourteenth birthday, Alyssa Lai, a California native of Chinese descent, received an offer of cosmetic surgery from her parents and grandmother: blepharoplasty. The procedure stitches a permanent fold in the upper eyelid to create a double-lidded and rounder appearance. Alyssa's mother and father felt that she would be "prettier" this way, but she ultimately declined the offer. "To be beautiful, you don't have to look beautiful in a Caucasian sense,"[1] Lai says.

Still, blepharoplasty remains popular among Asians, of whom 50 percent are born with a single eyelid, a distinctive feature of the ethnic group. In fact, blepharoplasty is the top cosmetic procedure in Asia, with a price tag of about $2,500. As common as it is, eyelid surgery is vigorously opposed among members of the Asian American community. "It's terrible that global culture has made the Western standard of beauty so predominant that Asian women feel they have to go under the knife to achieve that standard,"[2] asserts Dina Gan, an Asian American author and journalist. Other critics view it as an act of self-mutilation. "Double eyelid surgery is unnatural and people who do it are buying into a beauty myth that is not Asian based,"[3] contends Martin Wong, editor of Asian pop culture magazine *Giant Robot*.

In contrast, practitioners of the procedure insist that the majority of Asians who have blepharoplasty do not want to look Caucasian. "From having performed surgery since 1981, and teaching the surgical techniques to other doctors for the same period, I honestly do not believe that most of the Asian

1. Sandy Cobrin, "Asian-Americans Criticize Eyelid Surgery Craze," Womens eNews, August 15, 2004. www.womensenews.org.

2. Shirley Lin, "In the Eye of the Beholder?" AlterNet, March 6, 2001. www.alternet.org.

3. Sarah Matthews, "Asian Double Eyelid Surgery—Looking Brighter," July 19, 2009. http://guidetoplasticsurgery.com.

patients are wanting to look like Westerners or their Caucasian friends,"[4] proposes William P. Chen, a plastic surgeon based in Southern California. "Rather, they want to retain their Asian features with the addition of an aesthetically pleasing Asian eyelid crease, just like their Asian friends or siblings." In the following chapter, the authors deliberate how cosmetic surgery shapes beauty ideals, identity, and emotional well-being.

4. Frequently Asked Questions, Asian Eyelid Surgery Center, www.asianeyelid.com.

> "What you want to hear is that the teenager wants the surgery for [himself or herself]."

# Cosmetic Surgery Can Benefit Some Teens

**Richard D'Amico, as told to Matthew Shulman**

*Richard D'Amico is the former president of the American Society of Plastic Surgeons. Matthew Shulman is a writer for* U.S. News & World Report. *In the following viewpoint, D'Amico and Shulman discuss what makes a teenager a good candidate for cosmetic surgery. D'Amico recommends that several factors must be considered in determining whether it is appropriate for a teen: if he or she understands the nature of the procedure, has a personal desire for it, realistic expectations, and good self-esteem. Also, D'Amico states that reconstructive surgery for deformities and developmental problems can be wholly justified for youths under eighteen.*

As you read, consider the following questions:

1. How does D'Amico distinguish one group of teenage surgery candidates from other teens?

2. What is D'Amico's position on liposuction for adolescents?

3. What main considerations should parents and children take into account before choosing cosmetic surgery, as stated by D'Amico?

As millions of teenagers begin their final summer before college, not a few are prepping for cosmetic surgery, to take advantage of the long recovery time and a transition from one peer group to the next. In the aftermath of a $20 million-plus court award in Pennsylvania in May [2008] to a family whose 18-year-old daughter died from what was likely a pulmonary embolism after liposuction, some parents may be wondering whether cosmetic treatments in teens are safe.

*U.S. News & World Report* asked Richard D'Amico, president of the American Society of Plastic Surgeons, what families should consider when deciding whether to take the plunge.

## A Family and Personal Matter

*[U.S. News & World Report:] How do doctors determine if surgery in teens is appropriate?*

[Richard D'Amico:] I think it's important to draw a distinction between teenagers who are younger than 18 and those who are older. At 18, these individuals are adults in the eyes of the law and are allowed to make the decision on their own. For those under 18, it becomes a family and parental matter. We also have to distinguish between procedures that are purely cosmetic and those that are reconstructive. Several factors are important in deciding when and for whom surgery is appropriate: an ability to understand the procedure; that the desire for surgery does not reflect what a parent, friend, or boyfriend desires; and that expectations are realistic.

If your expectations aren't realistic and you have low self-esteem or no friends, cosmetic surgery is not the right answer. Rather, I would recommend counseling. But if a young person has good self-esteem and good family support, can understand what's going on, and has realistic expectations, then surgery may be appropriate. The need to know all these things is what makes the consultation so critical.

It can be entirely appropriate for teenagers under 18 to undergo reconstructive procedures. This is most often for maldevelopment of the breast in girls [which can include deformities and severe underdevelopment of the breasts and nipples] and overdevelopment of the breast in young teenage boys—a condition known as gynecomastia. When girls' breasts are too big for their bodies, a breast reduction is also considered a reconstructive procedure.

*What about cosmetic or aesthetic procedures?*

On the cosmetic side for those under 18, we're really talking about rhinoplasty, where the primary endeavor is to improve the appearance of the nose, whether or not there is a problem with the septum. Both the Food and Drug Administration [FDA] and the American Society of Plastic Surgeons feel that young women under 18 should not get breast implants for purely cosmetic reasons.

Once a teenager reaches 18 years of age, we can perform cosmetic enhancements or enlargement of the breast using saline implants. FDA guidelines suggest waiting until 22 years of age before using gel implants.

*Is it considered OK for teens who are concerned with their weight to get liposuction?*

It's generally discouraged in teens younger than 18 with weight problems. It's recommended that weight loss is addressed and controlled with diet and exercise. The body contouring technique is not a weight loss tool, and that is true at any age. In fact, if someone is grossly overweight, he or she has to get to a better weight before liposuction is considered.

There are a lot of teenagers with psychological issues related to their weight. And while as plastic surgeons we usually don't get involved in counseling, if someone who is 15 or 16 is obsessed with [his or her] weight, counseling can be very helpful.

*And for teens 18 and older?*

It's a very reasonable and useful tool, but we like to have people with the maturity to be able to manage their weight with diet and exercise. Then contouring improvements can be made.

*Are teenagers more susceptible to certain complications than adults are?*

No. But people need to know that cosmetic surgery is still surgery and, though extremely rare, there are risks. Before we even go ahead with surgery, the family and the teenager need to understand the potential risks from both surgery and anesthesia.

However, there are instances where the teenage body is still growing and we don't operate on structures if they need time for further growth. With rhinoplasties, the issue is usually that the nose is already too big, so further growth will not be beneficial.

## Consultation and Considerations

*Can you describe what happens at a typical consultation?*

When a teenager who is younger than 18 comes in for the consultation, he or she must be accompanied by a parent or guardian. We first sit down and discuss the patient's request—in this case it would almost always be rhinoplasty—and we make sure it's something the teenager actually wants. You can tell when people want something or if they're simply there because mom has expectations in the teenager's appearance. Those things come out in the discussion. We find out if the teenager's expectations are realistic and ask [him or her] point-blank why [he or she] wants the surgery. They have to be able to talk and communicate their desires and not just parrot what someone else told them.

If their reason is just that their boyfriends want it or because some friends tease them, then that's inappropriate and I wouldn't offer . . . the surgery. In that case, I would postpone the discussion until they're really ready. What you want to hear is that the teenager wants the surgery for [himself or herself]. And as we talk to [him or her], we determine what [his or her] self-esteem is.

*What then?*

If I don't think [he or she is] ready, I'll tell the parents that yes, there may be an issue with the teen's nose, but I don't think this young person is ready yet. Let's talk again next year. If the teenager believes that if only she got her nose done, she would no longer be ostracized, then I'd refer her for counseling. I also look at the level of parental support. You really have to look at personal maturity and make sure that the expectations are realistic. Certainly parents can seek a second opinion, but they must treat what the surgeon says very seriously.

*What are the main considerations a parent and teenager should take into account when deciding on plastic surgery?*

No matter what someone's age is, patients should always choose a plastic surgeon certified by the American Board of Plastic Surgery. The second critical element is to make sure the surgery is carried out in a licensed hospital or accredited facility because complications can happen to people of all ages.

Make sure you sit down with the plastic surgeon and have a thorough consultation that goes beyond just the area of concern, particularly with teenagers. This includes a thorough physical exam and all preoperative testing. The doctor should get to know the teenager and make sure he or she is emotionally ready and will be able to deal with complications if they come up. I see all of my patients twice before I do surgery, and I think it's a good idea to have the patient come back after the first discussion. It shows perseverance and drives home the point that this is a serious decision.

And if the patient is 18 and older, but still young, I encourage parents or guardians to be involved in the decision making, even though it is the patient's legal choice.

*"It's time to educate girls on the reality of going under the knife but even more so, it's time teens began feeling good about the bodies they have."*

# Teens Should Not Have Cosmetic Surgery

## Sabrina Joseph and Khorally Pierre

*Sabrina Joseph and Khorally Pierre were participants in Teen Voices, a journalism and media program for young women. In the following viewpoint, Joseph and Pierre urge their peers to resist the pressure to place themselves at the risks of cosmetic surgery. While the authors insist that reconstructive surgery is appropriate, they maintain that breast implants, which are growing in popularity, pose real and serious dangers to teenage girls. Moreover, Joseph and Pierre claim that female's bodies further develop in adulthood, and the desire to get larger breasts or other procedures disappears with maturity.*

As you read, consider the following questions:

1. How do the authors support their claim that more teenage girls are getting breast implants?

2. In the authors' view, what should a surgeon determine when a teen considers plastic surgery?

3. What are the cosmetic problems of breast implants, according to the authors?

Do you feel pressure to be flawless? Are you considering plastic surgery to achieve perfection? Think again! Plastic surgery is not all it's cut out to be—no pun intended!

Thousands of teen girls are going under the knife without knowing the risks. One of the most popular cosmetic procedures among girls is breast implants. What is it with big boobs anyway? Do girls feel bigger breasts lead to more attention? Teen Voices made it their mission to educate girls on the harsh reality of cosmetic surgery, particularly breast augmentation.

## What Is Plastic Surgery?

Plastic surgery is a special type of surgery that alters, repairs, or reconstructs a person's physical defects or features. There are two types of plastic surgery: reconstructive and cosmetic. People get plastic surgery for multiple reasons. Some get it to change parts of their body they are unsatisfied with while others undergo it for medical reasons.

Some medical conditions that might require plastic surgery include birth defects or traumatic injuries. Issues requiring reconstructive surgery may affect a person's daily life, causing them physical or psychological trauma. An example of a situation requiring reconstructive surgery includes breast implants after a woman has received a double mastectomy, a procedure by which both breasts are removed as a treatment for breast cancer. Implants are used to make the woman look like she has breasts again after they've been removed.

This isn't always why women and girls go under the knife. Many undergo cosmetic surgery to improve their looks and boost their self-confidence. Cosmetic surgery changes a part of the body a person is dissatisfied with. Breast augmentation, a type of cosmetic surgery, is one of the most popular procedures today and despite various risks, teen girls are opting to undergo surgery for bigger boobs.

## Growing Breasts and Growing Numbers

As the number of breast augmentation operations increase, so does the amount of teens going under the knife. The American Society of Plastic Surgeons reported last year that the number of teens under 18 years old who received breast implants between 2002 and 2003 nearly tripled from 3,872 to 11,326. According to the book *Our Bodies, Ourselves*, more than 300,000 women and teenagers reported having breast implants in 2008.

Many teens are even receiving plastic surgery as a high school graduation gift. Whereas many graduates pack up a beat-up Volvo and head to college, some recent graduates are arriving on campus with a new set of "headlights" at a cost of between $4,000 and $8,000 in the United States. "I think it's just becoming more and more common and mainstream," says Beth Katz, an intern at Our Bodies, Ourselves, a non-profit organization that provides information on women's health. "As the numbers go up for the rest of the population, the numbers go up for teens as well. You see it in the media, everyone's getting breast implants," Katz says.

If you are considering breast implants, it is important to know and understand the legal aspects. The Food and Drug Administration banned breast augmentation for those under 18 unless it is for reconstructive purposes, and those between the ages of 18 and 22 can only have the option of saline-filled breast implants rather than the controversial silicone-filled implants.

## Why Are Teens Getting Breast Implants?

Why are teens opting to have plastic surgery? Why can't we just be happy with the way we look? "I think a lot of it has to do with the media and everything that teens see in the media with big breasts being associated with beauty. Teens especially are always willing to make themselves feel better and feel more confident," says Katz.

No one is perfect though; after all, what is perfection? Oftentimes, flaws make people unique and beautiful! "Girls sharing their story about being imperfect and everyone openly talking about [what they feel their imperfections are] would help," says Katz. Teens such as Christina Joseph, 16, have a similar opinion. "Breast implants are a waste of time, especially for girls that are under 18 years old. You should love your body and take care of it because you'll have it for the rest of your life. So why waste time and money paying for a surgery that changes the real you?"

Before many plastic surgeons operate, they not only question their teens but also have them undergo psychological testing to determine whether or not they are mature enough to make this decision. Teens are asked various questions including, "Why do you want to do the surgery?" so the surgeon can find out the teen's motivation. Surgeons also check to make sure patients don't have any personality disorders that might negatively influence their decision to get plastic surgery. Still there are no guidelines requiring plastic surgeons to analyze or discuss the choice with their patients.

## Risks and Implants Gone Wrong

Katz advises teens to "look into all of the health risks beforehand and to be prepared to deal with the consequences. If they do decide to go with it, they should continue checking to make sure that the breast implants aren't hurting their health as they get older."

Some of the risks of breast implants include infection, chronic breast pain, breast or nipple numbness, capsular contracture (when the immune system rejects the implant), breakage and leakage, and necrosis (when the body tissue around the implant dies). These issues may require additional surgery. Other risks include "cosmetic" problems with the way the breasts look, such as an abnormal nipple. Some women are dissatisfied with their implants because they don't look natural or their saline-filled implants make sloshing sounds (breastimplantinfo.org).

Implants can also affect other areas of women's health. Some women might have problems breastfeeding after undergoing augmentation. According to the National Cancer Institute, breast implants have been linked to causing cancer and interfering with mammograms, a type of screening that helps detect breast cancer. Kacey Long received saline implants at 19 and suffered from chronic fatigue, loss of hair, muscle tremors, dizziness, memory disturbances and other symptoms. A spokesperson against saline implants, she had them removed and is still recovering from both the financial blow and the debilitating symptoms. "I am seeing a doctor who specializes in treating damaged muscles, nerves and joints. I also regularly visit a chiropractic and acupuncture specialist," she writes on her Web site (www.implantsout.com). She is currently creating an organization to educate women on the risks of saline implants.

Many women find their breasts grow more in their late teens and early twenties, and the self-consciousness that may have driven them to originally seek surgery tends to wane as time goes on. "They cause a lot of serious health risks that people don't usually mention and they're especially bad in teens that are still growing," says Katz. "In terms of self-esteem and self-confidence for teens, I don't think breast implants are the way to get that. It's about learning to accept and love the bodies that you have."

The risks of cosmetic surgery for girls under the age of 18 are undeniably high. It's time to educate girls on the reality of going under the knife but even more so, it's time teens began feeling good about the bodies they have.

> *"It seems clear that a lessening of ethnic characteristics (rather than a 'refining'—whatever that means) is what is going on."*

# Ethnic Characteristics Should Be Considered Prior to Cosmetic Surgery

*Amy Wilentz*

*In the following viewpoint, Amy Wilentz claims that many cosmetic surgeries performed on ethnic patients conform to a Westernized beauty standard: a slimmer nose, pronounced chin, and widened eyes with double lids. The number of nonwhite patients electing cosmetic surgery—in the United States and around the world—is rising fast, Wilentz contends, and the procedures favor a Caucasian look. Both surgeons and patients alike insist that physical ideals are becoming multiracial, but Wilentz counters that celebrity and fashion cultures have narrowed these ideals. Wilentz is an author and teaches literary journalism at the University of California, Irvine.*

As you read, consider the following questions:

1. What is the cultural debate that surrounds plastic surgery, in Wilentz's opinion?

2. In Wilentz's view, what drives the cosmetic surgery craze around the world?

3. What is the author's position on wider accessibility and acceptance of cosmetic surgery?

All over the world, to paraphrase [writer] Dorothy Parker's observation about singer Fanny Brice's plastic surgery, people are cutting off their noses to spite their race.

They are doing it everywhere, but the front lines are probably in Beverly Hills. On any given weekday in the offices of Dr. Paul Nassif on Spalding Drive, men and women, teenagers to 50-year-olds, wait in a luxuriously carpeted and upholstered reception area. On a comfortable chair, a young African American woman in her 20s reads a book. An older Asian woman in a broad hat emerges from the consulting rooms. A Latina chats with the receptionist. The door to the outer hallway opens and in comes a perfect Hollywood blonde in a lacy white blouse, white linen trousers, gold bracelets, diamonds on her fingers, a designer handbag hanging from her shoulder. An older white man leaving the office jokes with a nurse: "Now I'm ready for a weekend of golf." On a closed-circuit television in a corner, testimonials by former patients and video footage of procedures play to current and prospective clients.

The patients are ethnically diverse. What many have in common, of course, is a desire to appear more youthful. But page through the before-and-after album that lies on a waiting room table and you see the other trend.

In this office it's known as Westernization.

Here is a 31-year-old Asian woman who "feels that her nose is too bulbous."

Procedure: Westernization rhinoplasty. Comment: "Notice the smoother, softer nose with a 'natural' appearance." Next, a 26-year-old African American male "desiring a 'Westernization' rhinoplasty . . . he has an ethnic nose and wants it thinner and desires more projection." Comment: "Notice the improved but not overcorrected profile with more projection and a slimmer nasal tip. His nostrils also were narrowed with a natural appearance." Over on this page, "a 25-year-old Middle Eastern male desiring removal of the hump on his nose."

While all this Westernization is going on, the cautionary example of Michael Jackson remains on people's minds. Patients and doctors say he is often mentioned as they discuss plans for surgery. No one wants to make his mistakes; no one wants to turn into a monster of tragic racial confusion.

Both doctors and patients say the lessons of multiculturalism learned in the 1970s and 1980s have had a significant impact on the practice of cosmetic surgery. . . . Dr. Charles Lee of Beverly Hills (not of Spalding Drive, but of Roxbury Drive), whose patients are often Asian Americans, dislikes the word "Westernization."

"If I performed an operation to Westernize an Asian patient," Lee says, "they'd be unhappy because it would look unnatural. When I give someone a double eyelid, which is a very popular surgery among Asians today, I try to retain the Asian look of their eyes. I want to create a natural appearance, an Asian appearance. Ideas of beauty have evolved over a long time, and there is now an evolving standard that is transracial."

## The Politics of Appearance

There has always been a cultural debate surrounding cosmetic surgery. The debate swirls around such emotionally charged issues as God-givenness and individual free will. Should one bear for life a physical or mental burden that one was dealt at birth? What constitutes a physical defect? There are questions of masquerade and racial or ethnic passing, as well. Should people undergo procedures that make them less perceivably members of the socially stigmatized race or ethnic group into which they were born? Does an unconscious self-hatred, stemming from discrimination by a dominant culture, push people into the waiting rooms of cosmetic surgeons?

"It's all about the politics of appearance," says Patricia J. Williams, a Columbia professor and columnist for the *Nation* magazine. "It is distressing to see those who are getting cosmetic surgery trying to appear more Western European. Plastic surgery, which began as a process to reconstruct in medical emergencies, has been taken up by those who have been so oppressed that their ethnicity is perceived as a medical emergency."

That is one side of the debate. Cultural historian and Emory University professor Sander Gilman, who has written extensively on the cultural impact and significance of cosmetic surgery, represents another. He says critics like Williams can "end up sounding like Catholic cardinals from the 17th century. Their implicit argument is that you must suffer with it, because it is God's will. Aesthetic standards, however, are not absolutes, but rather questions of negotiation and accommodation within a culture and among individuals. I think that one must be careful not to assume that self-hatred is always the motivation behind the patient's desire for surgery. For example, by the 1970s here, the idea wasn't not to look Jewish—but not to look too Jewish."

In the late 1800s, a German Jewish surgeon named Jacques Joseph (he had changed his name from Jakob Joseph) developed many of the non-scarring techniques followed in present-day rhinoplasty. Scarring itself, as Gilman points out in his book *Making the Body Beautiful*, was controversial in Germany at the time. In order to advance in elite society, a man was better off if he could show certain racial scars inflicted during gentlemanly dueling. Joseph himself had such scars.

Indeed, some even had treatments to enhance the facial scars of swordsmanship.

Yet a Jew was better off socially if he had a straight nose (preferably by birth, but if not, by surgery) and no scarring to show that he had altered himself in order to pass. (In the late 18th century, syphilitic noses, eaten away by the venereal disease, were repaired with skin grafts taken from the patient's forehead; the scar there served as a sign of disease emblazoned on the patient's brow. Other non-venereal nose jobs were equally scarring, thus negating the value of the operation.)

Among German Jews, the cultural debate was this: Is it right to deny your Jewishness by changing your facial structure? Moreover, can cosmetic surgery really achieve what the patient is setting out to do? Will the non-Jew accept the Jew simply on the basis of a straight nose? In other words, there was the distinct possibility that cosmetic surgery was both morally wrong and wouldn't achieve the desired goal. Once Joseph perfected his non-scarring techniques, however, the nose job was more willingly accepted by his Jewish patients. Yet nose job or no, the Nazis were later quite able to isolate and identify the Jewish population. What then was the value of the cosmetic operation?

Let's be real. The history of plastic surgery, with its references to venereal disease and genocide, can seem a little . . . heavy . . . when you're sitting in a Beverly Hills waiting room on a nice spring day in the year 2006 waiting for a Botox injection. Like, don't harsh my buzz, dude; I got my hair done, too. I just wanna look good for the after-party tonight. The truth is that cosmetic surgery today is almost as accepted as makeup application, hair treatment and orthodontia. Since 1997, there has been a 444% increase in the number of cosmetic procedures in the U.S., according to the American Society for Aesthetic Plastic Surgery. Surgical operations have increased 119% since then, while nonsurgical, minimally invasive

interventions such as Botox injections, laser hair removal, acid wrinkle fillers, and skin abrasions and peels have shot up 726%.

## Ethnic Revision

This is not, as one might suspect, purely the result of a baby-boom generation that wants to cling unwrinkled to the word "baby." The desire for what might be called "ethnic revision" has helped pump up cosmetic surgery numbers. In the U.S. in 2005, the number of ethnic patients opting for cosmetic surgery rose about 65%, with almost 2.3 million procedures performed. In the U.S. last year, some 20% of all cosmetic procedures were performed on ethnic or racial minorities, according to the society. Latinos underwent more than 921,000 procedures, the largest number for any ethnic group, followed by African Americans, with 769,000. Both of these ethnic groups saw a 67% rise in the number of procedures over 2004, while Asian cosmetic surgery rose 58%.

The phenomenon is global. According to the International Society of Aesthetic Plastic Surgery, the number of cosmetic surgical procedures performed worldwide has increased 15% to 20% each year over the last five years. National types of beauty apparently no longer hold sway, with all continents lurching madly toward an improved, modified, Aryanized look—a Westernized face with a narrower, more protruding chin; a higher-bridged, more slender nose; smaller, narrower, downward-facing nostrils; and wider eyes with double lids. (In China, the enormous upsurge in cosmetic surgery has taken place both in hospitals and in small back-alley shops called "beauty-science centers." Not surprisingly, this boom has caused an uptick in lawsuits against cosmetic surgery practitioners, with an estimated 200,000 such filings in the last 10 years.)

In many ways, the American entertainment industry has fueled the craze, first by beaming images of the dominant world culture to a global audience and then by offering television shows that make cosmetic surgery seem less dangerous and less stigmatizing than it used to be. *Dr. 90210* and *Extreme Makeover*, which depict patients undergoing reconstructive procedures, have expanded the population interested in cosmetic surgery from a small, elite minority to one of millions. *Extreme Makeover* airs in more than 100 countries.

There is a famous joke about nose jobs that no longer holds true but is instructive in explaining the trend in ethnic cosmetic surgery. It's about a New York–area woman who had a nose job as a teenager. One day, she's walking down the street with her husband in Paris, or Rome, or London, and she sees another woman walking toward her. "Look," she shouts at her husband, clutching his arm and pointing, "a Dr. Diamond nose!"

Howard Diamond of Manhattan was a real person, a master plastic surgeon who probably performed more nose jobs than any other in his field in the 1960s and 1970s. It has been said that all the noses Diamond did ended up looking the same: cookie-cutter noses, or assembly-line noses. In the joke, "Dr. Diamond" is simply the name that stands for all plastic surgeons of his era, when the nose job was king. Many of the real Diamond's colleagues and patients deplore this besmirching of his reputation.

Still, there is no question that rhinoplasty in the '60s and '70s produced hundreds of pinched, ski-slope noses intended to look like the adorable button nose of a Barbie doll or a Cheryl Tiegs, a top fashion model of the era.

No longer. Indeed, many of the postoperative noses fixed today by Nassif and other plastic surgeons have flaws very much like the ones "Dr. Diamond" was called in to correct. "I'm not making people similar," Nassif says. "If you take 10 of my African American patients and put them in a room together, they will not look alike."

On Spalding Drive in Beverly Hills, patients don't want their names printed, but they aren't shy. A Latina explains that when she had her nose "fixed" in the 1980s, the doctor did an awful job. "It looked terrible, and it didn't even work properly! And when I finally went to have it redone, I did not want to look like anything but my own race. That first time, I didn't know what to say, what to ask for, I was so young. But now I knew: I still wanted to look Hispanic. And the revision was good. The doctor returned my look to a natural look; he returned my ethnicity to me so that now I have something that looks like I was born with it. I never wanted to look cutesy or . . . Caucasian. I wanted to have my mother's nose—my mother has a perfect nose."

Another rhinoplasty patient, this one Afro Caribbean, thinks Westernization isn't the right word for what's happening. "After all, there are plenty of Africans who have straight, narrow noses—look at the Ethiopians. I went from a wider to a narrower nose, but I did not want an arrow-straight nose. I wanted a nose that was in proportion to my small face. And my family and friends, when it was done, they couldn't even tell—they thought I'd lost weight. Somehow I looked better, but why they could not say. I always wanted it to look like me, only enhanced."

## A Desire for Conformity

In his main office in Beverly Hills, and at satellite offices in various parts of town, Dr. Lance Wyatt has a diverse patient population that includes Persian Jews, Latinos and African Americans. "What I really enjoy is the mix," Wyatt says, challenging Westernization. "You simply cannot assume that because a patient wants rhinoplasty, he's going to want a European nose. That may have been the assumption of physicians in yesteryear, but it's certainly not the assumption today. With the heterogenous mix we have here in L.A., and the vast number of interracial couples, you have to appreciate the specific ethnic standards. The concept now is to retain and improve."

Wyatt says there is a give-and-take going on, a lot of play within ethnic stereotypes, so that in the past a Jewish woman would have been unlikely to ask for thicker lips or buttock enhancement, but she might do so now. His Middle Eastern patients come in and say: "I want lips like . . . yours, doctor."

Wyatt is African American, although he is quick to point out that he is of African, European and Native American descent. "And in this, I am not unusual," he says. "It's a beautiful thing about living in this fabulous city: You're exposed to people's ethnic characteristics every day. . . . My Jewish patients leave my office on their way out for a Mexican dinner; my Latino patients come in eating a bagel.

"The average person is getting ideas from what they see in the mass culture, coming out of Hollywood, television . . . but you can't forget that the elite that creates the mass culture here in L.A. are getting their ideas from what they see in our streets. . . . The mass culture is producing patients who say I want a Jennifer Lopez behind, Angelina Jolie lips, Pamela Anderson breasts and Halle Berry's nose."

Still, an observer—noting that most people go from wide noses to narrow, from hooked noses to straight, from flat noses to raised-bridge noses, from wide Asian faces to thinner-cheeked faces, from wide hips to narrower hips—can't quite banish the thought that someone is being fooled here.

Is it that the doctors and patients are suffering from a kind of mass Stockholm syndrome in which they don't realize that they have accepted the beauty standards of the dominant culture, of which Michael Jackson is the most prominent cosmetic victim? It seems clear that a lessening of ethnic characteristics (rather than a "refining"—whatever that means) is what is going on. In the days of Dr. Joseph of Berlin, if a Jewish rhinoplasty patient had asserted that he wanted to "refine" his nose but retain his Jewish ethnicity, other Jews would have laughed.

Here in the U.S., our Hollywood- and New York-bred celebrity/fashion culture has infected us with what seems to be an adolescent desire for conformity (to which even celebrities must hew). Forgotten is the idea that variety is the spice of life. Anyone, no matter his or her background, can imagine being a potential postoperative star.

Maybe the trend is good, in that it has the potential to make us all equals, each looking more or less like the other. Many have argued that the widespread acceptance of cosmetic surgery represents a new kind of democracy. Carried to its extreme, the trend would level the physical field and make each generation a brave new postoperative world. In that world of beauties, we could all compete for Orlando Bloom or Kate Bosworth. But as Charles Darwin wrote, "If every one were cast in the same mould, there would be no such thing as beauty."

> "The increased suicide risk—together with a similar increase in deaths from alcohol or drug dependence—suggests that plastic surgeons should consider mental health screening and follow-up for women who seek breast implants."

# People Who Seek Plastic Surgery Should Have Mental Health Screenings

*Newsmax.com*

*In the following viewpoint, Newsmax.com reports that women who undergo breast augmentation are more likely to suffer from psychiatric disorders and are at risk for suicide. Findings from a study in the August 2007* Annals of Plastic Surgery *demonstrate the link between breast implants and a high risk of suicide. The viewpoint asserts that plastic surgeons should consider mental health screenings for potential patients. Newsmax.com is a leading independent news site that focuses on personal health, politics, and breaking news.*

As you read, consider the following questions:

1. According to the viewpoint, how much higher was the suicide rate for women with breast implants?
2. At what age was the suicide risk greatest for women? How much greater?
3. According to the viewpoint, the true rates of psychological problems among women with cosmetic implants are much higher. Why?

The long-term risk of suicide is tripled for women who have undergone cosmetic breast implant surgery, concludes a study in the August [2007] *Annals of Plastic Surgery*, published by Lippincott Williams & Wilkins, a part of Wolters Kluwer Health. This long-term study further confirms the link between breast implants and a strikingly high risk of suicide and other related causes of death.

The increased suicide risk—together with a similar increase in deaths from alcohol or drug dependence—suggests that plastic surgeons should consider mental health screening and follow-up for women who seek breast implants according to the new study, led by Loren Lipworth, ScD, of the International Epidemiology Institute in Rockville, Md., and the Vanderbilt University Medical Center, Nashville, Tenn.

Dr. Lipworth and colleagues performed an extended follow-up study of 3,527 Swedish women who underwent cosmetic breast implant surgery between 1965 and 1993. Death certificate data were used to analyze causes of death among women with breast implants, compared to the general female population.

## Higher Suicide Rate

At an average follow-up of nearly 19 years, the suicide rate was three times higher for women with breast implants, compared to the general population (based on 24 deaths among implant recipients). The risk was greatest—nearly seven times higher—for women who received their breast implants at age 45 or older. (The average age at breast implant surgery was 32 years.)

Suicide risk was not significantly increased for the first ten years after implant surgery. After that, however, suicide risk increased with time since surgery—risk was 4.5 times higher from 10 to 19 years' follow-up, and six times higher after 20 years.

Women with breast implants also had higher rates of death from psychiatric disorders, including a three-fold increase in deaths resulting from alcohol and drug dependence. Several additional deaths, classified as accidents or injuries, might have been suicides or involved psychiatric disorders or drug/ alcohol abuse as a contributing cause. "Thus at least 38 deaths (22% of all deaths) in this implant cohort were associated with suicide, psychological disorders, and/or drug and alcohol abuse/dependence," the researchers write.

There was no increase in the risk of death from cancer, including breast cancer, among women with breast implants. Increases in deaths from lung cancer and respiratory diseases such as emphysema likely reflected higher smoking rates among women with breast implants.

Several epidemiological studies have found an increased suicide rate among women with cosmetic breast implants. The current study provides extended follow-up data on a previous nationwide study of Swedish women with breast implants, more than doubling the number of deaths analyzed. The use of Swedish national health care and death certificate records ensures near-complete identification of women undergoing breast implant surgery and information on causes of death.

## Psychiatric Problems in Cosmetic Surgery Patients

The increases in suicide and in deaths related to alcohol and drug dependence suggest that a "nontrivial proportion of

# Observing Office Behavior

Patients' behavior during their office visits should be observed closely. A 30-minute to 45-minute consultation is a relatively brief period of time to assess patients' psychological functioning. Patients typically are on their best behavior during their initial consultation and will often expend a great deal of effort to present themselves to the surgeon as "appropriate" for surgery. Important psychosocial information may be withheld if patients believe that it may result in rejection for surgery. Therefore, every bit of information obtained either during the consultation, or observed during interactions with the nursing or office staff, should be used in making a determination of appropriateness for surgery.

Nursing staff and office assistants, as compared to cosmetic surgeons, are in unique positions to gather important and potentially problematic information about patients. Members of the office staff often witness different aspects of patients' behavior during their interactions in the office. These behaviors can often suggest the presence of psychopathology that may interfere with the postoperative outcome.

Patients who have difficulty following the office routine warrant further attention. Those who frequently cancel or change appointments, ask for appointments outside of office hours, or who do not wish to talk to anyone other than the surgeons should be reconsidered for surgery. Patients who raise concerns among the staff should, as a minimum, be seen for a second preoperative consultation. If concerns persist, these patients should be referred to a psychologist or psychiatrist for a consultation.

*Michael S. Kaminer, Kenneth A. Arndt, and Jeffrey S. Dover,*
Atlas of Cosmetic Surgery. *2nd ed.*
*Philadelphia, PA: Saunders, 2009.*

women undergoing breast augmentation ... may bring with them—or develop later—serious long-term psychiatric morbidity and eventually mortality," Dr. Lipworth and colleagues write. Since the study includes only deaths, the true rates of psychological and substance abuse problems among women with cosmetic implants are likely much higher. The researchers conclude, "Such findings warrant increased screening, counseling, and perhaps post-implant monitoring of women seeking cosmetic breast implants."

In an invited discussion, David B. Sarwer, PhD, associate professor of psychology at the University of Pennsylvania School of Medicine, recommends that plastic surgeons assess the mental health status and history of women desiring breast augmentation. In addition to mood disorders such as depression, screening should focus on body image disorders, such as body dysmorphic disorder [a psychological disorder in which a person obsesses about a perceived physical flaw]. "In cases where the patient is currently in mental health treatment, the surgeon should contact the mental health professional to confirm that the patient is psychiatrically stable and appropriate for surgery at this time," Dr. Sarwer writes. "[U]ntil we know more about the relationship between breast implants and suicide, this conservative approach is recommended with both the patient's and surgeon's well-being in mind."

# Periodical Bibliography

*The following articles have been selected to supplement the diverse views presented in this chapter.*

Dan Bilefsky            "If Plastic Surgery Won't Convince You, What Will?" *New York Times*, May 24, 2009.

Robert Burton           "How Looks Can Kill," *Salon*, January 31, 2008.

Ruth Charny             "The Many Faces of Plastic Surgery," *WowO Wow.com*, June 17, 2009. www.wowowow.com.

Laura T. Coffey         "Can Plastic Surgery Be Good for Teens?" TODAY Parenting, March 30, 2010. http://today.msnbc.msn.com.

Jennifer                "Extreme Makeover: Feminist Edition," *Ms.*, Cognard-Black    Summer 2007.

Ann Geracimos           "Ethnic Cosmetic Surgeries Rising," *Washington Times*, September 10, 2008.

Sheila Hall and Karen   "Getting a Handle on Patient Education," *Plastic Surgery Practice*, May 2010. Zupko

Cara Kulwicki           "The Racism of Cosmetic Surgery," Curvature Blog, November 6, 2007. http://thecurvature.com.

Mary Brophy Marcus      "Cosmetic Surgeries: What Children Will Do to Look 'Normal,'" *USA Today*, June 25, 2009.

Mark Roth               "In an Instant, Their Faces Were Gone," *Pittsburgh Post-Gazette*, July 25, 2010.

Valerie Ulene           "Plastic Surgery for Teens," *Los Angeles Times*, January 12, 2009.

CHAPTER 3

# Why Do People Have Cosmetic Surgery?

# Chapter Preface

In January 2010, reality television star Heidi Montag appeared on the cover of *People* after having ten cosmetic procedures and treatments in one day: a mini brow lift; Botox injections in her forehead and frown lines; a second nose job; fat injections in her lips, cheeks, and laugh lines; buttocks augmentation; a second breast augmentation; a chin reduction; liposuction on her neck; liposuction on her thighs, waist, and hips; and her ears pinned back. "I would say the biggest reason is to feel better, to feel perfect,"[1] Montag revealed to *People* about her motivations. "I was an ugly duckling before." She was also set to release her first pop album, insisting that "it's a superficial industry."

Montag did not have a shortage of detractors. *Newsweek* listed eleven things it found disturbing about her quest for physical perfection, from her insistence that her nipped and tucked self is the "real" her to conforming to a sexist standard of beauty. Actress Emmy Rossum took to Twitter and argued, "By putting this on magazine covers, we are somehow legitimizing the dangerous lengths to which some will go for fame and 'beauty.'"[2] Also, Margaret Hartmann on the Jezebel blog blasted *People* and other magazines "that reward [Montag] with fame and publish photos for the public to scrutinize every inch of her more 'perfect' body."[3]

Others, nonetheless, came to Montag's defense and her personal choices. Oliver Miller of the PopEater blog contended that criticisms of her cosmetic surgeries were hypocritical. "We relentlessly gossip about and mock male and

1. Jennifer Garcia, "Heidi Montag Obsessed with Being 'Perfect,'" *People*, January 25, 2010.

2. Jezebel, "Just Perfect: *People* Glamorizes Plastic Surgery Addiction," January 14, 2010. http://jezebel.com.

3. Ibid.

female celebrities who become in any way less attractive,"[4] he declared. "And then we act all surprised when celebrities become overly concerned with their looks." Comedy veteran Joan Rivers, who is not shy about going under the knife, sympathized with Montag's attempt to boost her music career by enhancing her appearance. "You show me anyone that walked down that red carpet at the Grammys that didn't have something done to them at one point. Everyone just lies to your face,"[5] Rivers told *Access Hollywood*. "It's a business where you have to look good." In the following chapter, the authors probe the social, psychological, and personal aspects that influence individuals to alter their faces and bodies.

4. PopEater, "In Defense of Heidi Montag: Live and Let Lipo," January 19, 2010. www .popeater.com.

5. *Access Hollywood*, "'I Feel Very Sorry' for Heidi Montag," www.accesshollywood.com.

*"Most of my patients don't choose to have surgery for the superficial reasons that come first to mind but because they are in search of something else more profound."*

# Most People Do Not Have Cosmetic Surgery for Vanity

*Loren Eskenazi*

*In the following viewpoint excerpted from* More than Skin Deep: Exploring the Real Reasons Why Women Go Under the Knife, *Loren Eskenazi supports cosmetic surgery as a personal choice. She is troubled by its commoditization and treatment as a spectacle on reality television shows and by misperceptions that it is harmless compared to other forms of surgery. These factors, Eskenazi contends, undermine a genuine discussion about cosmetic surgery; in her experience as a practitioner and a patient, women who are emotionally healthy seek cosmetic surgery as a rite of passage, and through the experience, gain inner healing and transformation. Eskenazi is a cosmetic surgeon and breast reconstruction expert.*

Loren Eskenazi, "Chapter 1: Cosmetic Surgery and the Promise of Transformation," *More than Skin Deep: Exploring the Real Reasons Why Women Go Under the Knife*. New York: HarperCollins Publishers, 2007. Copyright © 2007 by Loren Eskenazi and Peg Streep. All rights reserved. Reproduced by permission of HarperCollinsPublishers Inc.

As you read, consider the following questions:

1. What is the future of cosmetic surgery, in Eskenazi's opinion?
2. What is Eskenazi's position on opponents' views of cosmetic surgery?
3. What does Eskenazi allege that her patients share in common?

Some twenty-five years ago, I went to medical school to become a healer. I chose plastic surgery because the transformation it offered patients was immediate and life-changing. As a young medical student, I witnessed cleft lips made whole, birth defects rectified, and missing body parts recreated, and I fell in love with the extraordinary promise offered by the specialty. I traveled to foreign countries as part of a surgical team that in real and visible ways altered the lives of hundreds of adults and children over the course of a few weeks. I saw that each life and each surgery was unique, and I felt sure and confident that this was medicine at its finest and most personally fulfilling.

Now, having performed roughly ten thousand surgeries and undergone three procedures myself, I spend my days as the founding partner in an all-women's practice in San Francisco, where I devote half my time to breast reconstruction after cancer and half to cosmetic surgery in all its forms. I now see that the healing we offer as surgeons isn't always as clear-cut as it once appeared, and that cosmetic surgery raises questions and concerns I didn't anticipate when I was just beginning.

I've grown troubled as cosmetic surgery increasingly becomes, with each passing year, a commodity in American life, a readily available answer to dissatisfaction with all aspects of the physical self. Where it was once the province of the rich and famous, it's been fully democratized. It no longer needs to be done in Beverly Hills or Manhattan or cost a fortune, and more and more women each year from all over the country are choosing it. Information about procedures as well as local advertising from doctors offering their services [is] readily available on the Internet, testifying to the ubiquity of this surgery. Type in "cosmetic surgery" on Google and you'll get more than 1.5 million matches.

Each year, more and more American women elect to have cosmetic surgery, and the trend shows no sign of abating. More than 10 million surgical and nonsurgical procedures were performed on women in 2005, and by the time you read this, the number will undoubtedly be higher, as it has been with each passing year—a reflection of cosmetic surgery both as a cultural fact and a phenomenon. It has become a reliable growth business: In a single year—between 2003 and 2004—the number of abdominoplasties [tummy tucks] increased by 28 percent, the number of breast lifts 19 percent, the number of liposuctions 28 percent. In 2004 the number of breast augmentations went up 9 percent, and the abdominoplasties another 12 percent. This growth shows that cosmetic surgery has become just another product in our consumer society.

These are seismic changes and are having an effect on our culture and how we think about beauty, age, and our bodies. But we don't appear to have developed the philosophical tools we need to understand how these changes can help us live better and more fulfilled lives in the future or how these changes may, in the alternative, make personal happiness more elusive.

I actually had the opportunity to see how quickly attitudes toward cosmetic surgery changed when I participated in teaching a course in biomedical ethics at Stanford University in the early 1990s. I lectured undergraduates on body modification and plastic surgery for several years, and during that time, I witnessed an extraordinary shift in attitudes. The first year I taught, I asked my students if they would ever consider plastic surgery, and their answer was a resounding "No way!" They were judgmental about people who chose to alter their appearance. The second year, the answer was still a categorical no, but this time, a number of students knew someone who had had surgery and they were mildly curious about the possible benefits plastic surgery could bestow. Astonishingly, by the third year, one-half of the class answered that they would, indeed, opt for surgical improvement, although they remained troubled by how plastic surgery had the potential to install uniform standards of beauty in a culture. By the fourth year, when I asked the question, the class was solidly, in favor of cosmetic surgery and said they would absolutely avail themselves of it; their only caveat was cost. In fact, by then, they thought it should be covered by health insurance. For better or worse, young people are more flexible than their elders.

For our children and their children, cosmetic surgery will actively shape how our culture defines feminine beauty, assesses physical "perfection," and responds to the process of aging. In the face of a growing demand for the improvement and refinement of the physical characteristics we're born and age with, my profession will continue to be motivated to seek out new techniques, which will, in turn, bring in more patients. In the future, we'll be seeing the patient pool—now concentrated between the ages of thirty-six and sixty-four, with the majority of women between forty-five and fifty-five—get younger as procedures are performed earlier to stave off the early signs of aging and as "proactive" surgery becomes the norm.

While this should make me feel good about a wise career choice, it gives me pause.

As a woman, a doctor, and a patient, I feel we've reached an important watershed moment. Contradictions abound when it comes to cosmetic surgery. First, for all that Americans seem fascinated by and drawn to the promise or improvement that cosmetic surgery offers, they also believe that those who choose it are weak and insecure. Even as scientific research begins to decipher the complex relationship between the mind and the body, popular culture continues to insist that the mind and the body are separate and that the "mind" is morally superior to the body. What this means in practical terms is that women who choose to have cosmetic surgery for reasons that might be healthy and self-affirming will nonetheless be stereotyped as vain or overly concerned with appearance. As a result, there's no dialogue about how changing the body can and does change the "self" or the mind—even though there is plenty of scientific evidence at hand.

At the same time, there's a dangerous trend in the media to minimize the risks associated with surgery and to de-emphasize the rigors of recovery. In fact, surgery changes us in profound ways that go far beyond the results we see on the surface and should therefore never be trivialized.

So-called "reality" shows such as *The Swan, Extreme Makeover, I Want a Famous Face*, and *Dr. 90210* have contributed to both trends in significant ways. On the one hand, they have brought the promise offered by cosmetic surgery into the American mainstream, but on the other, by presenting it as theater or spectacle with exaggeratedly needy and desperate participants, they have only reinforced the stereotypes of the women who choose it. More dangerously, they suggest that multiple procedures performed weeks apart were actually performed on a single day and carry no extra risk. (Even *People* magazine asked the obvious question in its headline after 10 million people tuned in for the last episode of *The Swan*: "Has TV plastic surgery gone too far? Sixteen women, 151 procedures: Is this a good thing?") Multiple procedures and what I would call "extreme" surgery, which leaves the woman looking nothing like herself, are neither healthy nor desirable, and that is precisely what these shows promote.

The promotion of supposedly "scarless" surgery (which *doesn't* exist) and the "weekend" face-lift also contributes to the public's misconceptions, as does the extensive use of "be-

fore" and "after" pictures, which suggests both that surgical results are more consistently predictable than they actually are
and that recovery is minimal. Research demonstrates that call-
ing elective surgery "cosmetic" has lulled Americans into be-
lieving that the surgery being performed is somehow less dangerous, less complicated, and requires less surgical skill than
either "plastic" or "reconstructive" surgery. The word *cosmetic*
seems to connect surgery with lipstick and hair dye—things
you can pick up at a drugstore that are perfectly "safe"—and
thus encourages people to think that "cosmetic" surgery entails less pain and a shorter recovery period. Needless to say,
"cosmetic," "plastic," and "reconstructive" surgeries are precisely the same in terms of risk and recovery.

I would say instead that elective surgery is an important
and potentially life-changing event that should *always* be carefully considered.

Finally, despite America's apparent embrace of cosmetic
surgery—the rising number of surgeries, the television programs, the magazine articles, the media attention—our cultural attitudes toward it remain deeply ambivalent. With the
sides drawn—those all for it on one side and those against on
the other—there doesn't seem to be a forum in the middle for
meaningful discussion about what changing yourself through
surgery entails.

As I see it, our ambivalence about cosmetic surgery and
our reluctance to talk about it openly and directly have three
related consequences. First, a percentage of women will continue to have cosmetic surgery for reasons that may be inher-
ently unhealthy but, in a consumer society where cosmetic
surgery is just another product, will remain unexamined and
unchallenged except for the most obvious of cases. (By obvious, I mean patients with body dysmorphic disorder [a psychological disorder in which a person obsesses about a perceived physical defect], who have a history of multiple
surgeries and, usually, a history of complaints against their

former plastic surgeons—all "red flags" for a doctor. Some of these women will emerge from surgery in worse shape than they were in before.) Second—and this is even more important—the women who actually choose cosmetic surgery for reasons that are self-affirming and positive will be effectively isolated by social criticism and will, in many cases, internalize that ambivalence. This has created a subculture of shame and gossip, which is most evident in the magazine articles and Web sites devoted to analyzing whether celebrities have had "work" done, but affects ordinary women as well. Finally, and most important, as a society we aren't coming to terms with the real ways in which surgery alters more than the surface of the body. Beyond the obvious physical changes it creates, surgery has always been and will continue to be a tool of great power.

What discussions we do have about cosmetic surgery—no matter which side we take—just skim the surface. The opponents of cosmetic surgery dismiss the idea that the transformation it offers could be anything other than superficial; they see women who choose cosmetic surgery as filled with self-loathing, insecurity, and vanity, or the unwitting dupes of a female-bashing and quick-fix culture. In the main, despite the increasing numbers of women choosing to alter themselves surgically, our culture remains distrustful of the impulse for many different reasons. In the end, as research has found, most men and women believe that women who have surgery are "more vain or insecure" than women who don't.

The proponents of cosmetic surgery, on the other hand, downplay the risks and minimize the fact that invasive surgery changes us in ways both predictable and not. They ignore the fact that many of the contemporary images of feminine beauty touted as "desirable" are hardly womanly, healthy, or, in fact, attainable by any means other than surgery, since the number of women born on the planet with oversized breasts and no other body fat can probably be counted with ease. They don't address the cultural double standards applied to aging in women and men. They do not acknowledge that *some* women will seek cosmetic surgery because they are overly focused on their looks, afraid of aging, trapped by unrealistic expectations of what a woman and her body "should" look like, or because of a host of other reasons that are more unhealthy than not. They discount the fact that seeing the body as a "project" that is the "ultimate expression of self"—a pattern discerned by historian Joan Jacobs Brumberg in adolescent girls and young women—isn't good for any woman, young or old.

Discussions about cosmetic surgery, both pro and con, are usually placed in the following contexts: the pressure our contemporary culture puts on women to be young and beautiful; our society's focus on scientific advancement ("If it can be done, do it!"); and our American passion for self-improvement in all its forms. And while these discussions can be interesting and even pertinent, they do little to help women understand the choices open to them or the impulses that drive them to make certain choices. . . .

For the last decade, I've started each cosmetic consultation with two key questions: "How long have you considered this procedure?" and "Why have you decided to have it now?" Over time, the answers to my questions revealed a common thread: Almost every patient electing surgery had undergone a major life change within the previous year or was anticipating one in the very near future. The life changes were varied—a birth, a divorce, a death, a marriage, a milestone birthday such as forty, fifty, or sixty, or a significant change in life circumstance—but the decision to have surgery was, I came to see, born out of a need to mark the event or transition physically or to have the outer body reflect an inner change that was already taking place. Although it may seem paradoxical, the majority of my patients use their surgery as an opportunity to heal and grow. . . .

As a surgeon, I have seen that healing can, indeed, come out of both kinds of surgery, and while the journey of a woman diagnosed with a life-threatening disease is importantly and radically different from that of a healthy woman, there are also meaningful similarities. This understanding came slowly over a period of years and required that I cast aside my own long-held ideas as well as the succinct but spiritually empty answers I learned during my years of medical school and training. I began to fathom how the decision to alter one's body was endowed with immense power and agency and how "healing" wasn't a synonym for "cure." My own experiences as a patient and my own concerns about whether I was healing or harming my patients in the cosmetic part of my practice led me to look for answers in more out-of-the-way places than my traditional medical training might have suggested.

If I hadn't been a woman in a largely male profession with largely female patients, if the issues pertaining to women and feelings of self-worth hadn't been important to me, if I hadn't been subject to the same cultural pressures as every other woman, or if I hadn't had a lifelong interest in the connection between mind and body, spirit and flesh, I might never have found the answers I did. Perhaps if my practice had been limited to purely reconstructive surgery, as I naively expected in medical school, there would have been no questions to answer.

Surgery—with its risks, its implicit and explicit surrender of control, its cutting and wounding, its recovery, and the marks and scars it leaves—is central to my understanding, which correlates our contemporary surgical alterations with ancient rites of passage and initiation practiced the world over. Throughout history, humankind has celebrated life stages and passages by marking the flesh, and has understood the alteration of the body as part of a larger spiritual experience that changes the mind or soul. My own realization that all surgery constitutes a rite of passage evolved out of my patients' stories, my own surgeries, and my lifelong interest in symbolism and ritual. And, once I understood this principle, I also saw that the steps of surgery are virtually identical to those of initiation rites. . . .

Most of my patients don't choose to have surgery for the superficial reasons that come first to mind but because they are in search of something else more profound. For them, taking on the risk that surgery entails is an essential part of the process of inner transformation, which they have already begun on their own.

*"People are more and more drawn into thinking that their identities and bodies are similarly plastic, flexible, liquid."*

# The Social Pressure to Have Cosmetic Surgery Has Increased

*Karen Donley-Hayes*

*In the following viewpoint, Karen Donley-Hayes purports that an extreme makeover culture is emerging. As procedures and techniques improve and become more affordable, cosmetic surgery has turned from luxury to a prerequisite in a society that emphasizes appearance over merit, Hayes contends. Additionally, global economic and technological forces, she states, promote disposability and constant upgrading; people pursue surgical enhancement to reinvent themselves and remain competitive. Hayes is a contributor to* Cosmetic Surgery Times, Dermatology Times, *and the* Journal of the American Medical Association.

As you read, consider the following questions:

1. How does Anthony Elliott compare cosmetic surgery to the economy and technology?

2. In Hayes's view, how have patients evolved into consumers?

3. What is Anthony Elliott's concern about makeover culture?

Advances in technology, communication, and science have blazed new trails in globalization, changing the face of commerce, economies, and how the world conducts business. These advances have also enabled changes to the faces of the world population—literally and figuratively.

Anthony Elliott, a professor of sociology at Flinders University, Adelaide, South Australia, visiting research chair at the Open University, U.K. [United Kingdom], and author of the book *Making the Cut: How Cosmetic Surgical Culture Is Transforming Our Lives*, lectures internationally on the topic, and says that globalization fundamentally impacts cultural and social issues. He contends that new information technologies and scientific/medical advances bear directly on people's expectations—not only pertaining to business and trade, but at personal levels, as well.

"This is nowhere better dramatized than in makeover culture," he tells *Cosmetic Surgery Times*. "In the same way that corporations can restructure their operations from one country to another overnight, or in the same manner that we can send e-mail around the planet at the click of a mouse, people are more and more drawn into thinking that their identities and bodies are similarly plastic, flexible, liquid."

Beauty, or the perception of beauty, is not relegated to Western vanity. The immediacy made possible by live media reveals that the pressure to "put the best face forward" is global. A good illustration of this is the controversial use of a lip-synced song in the opening ceremonies of the Summer Olympic Games in Beijing in August 2008. Because the beautiful voice of the child singer was not, in the estimation of some, equaled by a beautiful face, a "suitably attractive" child was selected to be the face the world saw when it heard the song.

## Trading Up

Professor Elliott feels that the speed and "short termism" promoted by the global electronic economy drives and enables "re-inventing" one's own self.

"The new economy, in which disposability is elevated over durability and plasticity over permanence, creates fundamental anxieties and insecurities that more and more people are seeking to resolve at the level of the body," he argues.

"Consumerism or what you could call 'self-commodification,' offers a better take on what is occurring—the financing of 'enhanced body parts' is now creeping into monthly credit card statements—but again this is not for me the core of what is driving the cosmetic reinvention craze."

Professor Elliott says that, at an international level, bodies today are pumped, pummeled, plucked, suctioned, stitched, shrunk and surgically augmented at an astonishing rate. At the core of this, he says, is a new economy that judges people less on their achievements, less of their records of success, and more and more on the willingness to adapt, to change, to transform themselves. "Plastic surgery provides the most seductive answer to the new socioeconomic dilemmas."

This "answer" has become so universally available—with financing options to make it accessible to the less financially enabled—that it [has] become as much an expectation as a luxury for some people.

As with anything that evolves so rapidly, the role of cosmetic surgery is not static, and it remains to be seen how the trend develops. Will we burn through this as a fad across the planet? Is there some surfeit in sight eventually, or are we just getting started? Professor Elliott feels that while "drastic plas-

## The Makeover Ethos

Makeover television programs have proliferated: *Extreme Makeover* pitches plastic surgery, diet, exercise, and improved grooming as the best means of self-transformation, while *What Not to Wear* offers wardrobe advice as the fastest way to a "new you." *Extreme Makeover Home Edition* and *Trading Spaces* suggest home improvement as a route to self-improvement. *Queer Eye for the Straight Guy* advocates a multifaceted makeover, everything from wardrobe and grooming to interior design and home entertaining tips are revamped. In many cases, these makeover television shows are organized on the premise of "the ambush": the person to be "made over" has not volunteered, rather his or her friends and family have "turned them in." *Ambush Makeover*, *What Not to Wear*, and *While You Were Out* all operate on this structure. While you might have thought you looked just fine, or that your home was pretty comfortable, the people closest to you have been making some rather different, even scathing, assessments. No one is ever completely safe from the critical gaze of a culture steeped in the makeover ethos.

*Micki McGee, Self-Help, Inc.:*
*Makeover Culture in American Life.*
*New York: Oxford University Press, 2005.*

tic" is not yet the norm, "It is central to the 'new economy'—that of the finance, service, and media sectors—and to that extent is held up in society as a utopian image of the future." If this is indeed the case, the years ahead may usher in a new global perception of success—economically, socially, aesthetically.

## Old meets new?

This all begs the question: Is the desire to "reinvent" one-self—to be younger, thinner, bigger-breasted, less wrinkled, flatter-waisted—a new need or desire—or a Pandora's box that modern, globally reaching communication and technology may have opened?

"What's actually new in the surge of today's Botox converts and liposuction addicts is the social composition of those undergoing the surgeon's knife," Professor Elliott says. "More and more, middle-class professionals are turning to plastic surgery in an effort to retain, or sometimes acquire, youthful looks. Gold-collar class professionals—from London to Singapore to Sydney—are the new cosmetic surgery addicts. The British Association of Aesthetic Plastic Surgeons, for example, reports that professionals have replaced celebrities as the dominant group choosing to reinvent themselves through cosmetic surgery."

## Keeping Up with the Joneses

In an interesting paradox, the global medical community has also changed its relationship with the patient—who, where cosmetic surgery is concerned, has evolved from a "patient" to a consumer, and where the relationship between the physician and his or her "client" becomes much more collaborative.

Not all that long ago, Professor Elliott says, "anyone who wanted cosmetic surgery would have been advised to seek therapy in the first instance. Today, by contrast, there is a widespread acceptance that cosmetic surgical culture is beneficial and even desirable. Especially for tough-minded, highly motivated professionals, to be surgically 'freshened up' provides an edge in the marketplace."

Professor Elliott expresses concern that technical and medical capability has far outpaced the philosophical and emotional components that should be integral to modifying the face one shows to the world. If success, financial or otherwise, can be measured aesthetically, where does that leave the value of autonomy?

"This social transformation has not been heralded by a shift in psychological understanding," he says. "It is, rather, symptomatic of a pervasive addiction to the ethos of instant self-reinvention. And the flip side of today's reinvention craze is fear of personal disposability."

> "For women who seek improvements in certain physical areas, plastic surgery can be a very positive experience."

# Cosmetic Surgery Can Improve Self-Esteem

*Rick Nauert*

*Rick Nauert is senior news editor of Psych Central, the largest and oldest mental health social network. In the following viewpoint, the author asserts that cosmetic surgery can enhance women's self-esteem and sexuality, which health care practitioners must take into consideration. According to Nauert, a recent study shows a direct correlation between breast implants and reports of increased self-confidence and higher levels of sexual desire, arousal, and satisfaction. Nonetheless, he advises that cosmetic procedures are not a cure-all for these issues, and surgeons should be wary of patients with unrealistic expectations.*

As you read, consider the following questions:

1. How does Nauert characterize cosmetic surgery in the United States?
2. In Cynthia Figueroa-Haas's opinion, which women can benefit from cosmetic surgery?

Rick Nauert, "Plastic Surgery Helps Self-Esteem," Psych Central, March 23, 2007. Reproduced by permission.

3. How should nurses treat cosmetic surgery patients, according to the viewpoint?

Although the perception of women who undergo breast enlargement is often mixed, the recipients of the procedure often report a boost in self-esteem and positive feelings about their sexuality. A new study suggests health care practitioners should be cognizant that the elective procedure has positive psychological benefits.

Although plastic surgery should not be seen as a panacea for feelings of low self-worth or sexual attractiveness, it is important for health care practitioners to understand the psychological benefits of these procedures, says Cynthia Figueroa-Haas, a clinical assistant professor at University of Florida [UF] College of Nursing.

The findings—which revealed that for many women, going bigger is better—appear in the current issue of *Plastic Surgical Nursing*.

"Many individuals, including health care providers, have preconceived negative ideas about those who elect to have plastic surgery, without fully understanding the benefits that may occur from these procedures," said Figueroa-Haas, who conducted the study for her doctoral thesis at Barry University in Miami Shores before joining the UF faculty.

"This study provides the impetus for future studies related to self-esteem, human sexuality and cosmetic surgery."

In 2005, 2.1 million cosmetic surgical procedures were performed, according to the American Society for Aesthetic Plastic Surgery. That figure is expected to grow. Consider that the number of breast augmentation procedures alone increased a staggering 476 percent since 2000, according to the American Society of Plastic Surgeons.

More than 2 million women in the United States have breast implants, and this year [2007] more than 360,000 American women will undergo breast augmentation.

Figueroa-Haas studied 84 women who were 21 to 57 years old, assessing their perceptions of self-esteem and sexuality before and after cosmetic breast augmentation. Study participants had been previously scheduled for breast augmentation and were undergoing the procedure solely for cosmetic purposes. Eligible candidates were mailed a consent form, a demographic questionnaire and pre-tests asking them to rate their self-esteem and sexuality. They were then mailed a similar post-test two to three months after the surgery.

## Directly Correlated

Improvements in the women's self-esteem and sexual satisfaction were directly correlated with having undergone breast augmentation. Figueroa-Haas used two widely accepted scientific scales to measure self-esteem and sexuality, the Rosenberg Self-Esteem Scale and the Female Sexual Function Index, which assesses domains of sexual function, such as sexual arousal, satisfaction, experience and attitudes.

The participants' average self-esteem score increased from 20.7 to 24.9 on the 30-point Rosenberg scale, and their average female sexual function score increased from 27.2 to 31.4 on the 36-point index. Of note, after the procedure, there were substantial increases in ratings of sexual desire (a 78.6 percent increase from initial scores), arousal (81 percent increase) and satisfaction (57 percent increase). Figueroa-Haas did point out that a small number of participants showed no change in their levels of self-esteem or sexuality after surgery.

With a heightened interest in men's sexuality issues in recent years, the research sheds light on women's sexuality, and how plastic surgery can improve and enhance this important area of life, Figueroa-Haas said.

"So much attention is directed to men's sexuality issues; we have all seen countless commercials on drugs and therapy devoted to improving men's sexuality. Unfortunately, very little is discussed regarding women's sexuality issues," Figueroa-Haas said.

"I strongly believe that my research shows that interventions such as cosmetic plastic surgery can address these sorts of issues for some women. For example, those women who may have breast changes due to nursing or from the inevitable natural aging process. These women may not feel as attractive, which could ultimately negatively impact their levels of self-esteem and sexuality."

Figueroa-Haas warned that women should not view plastic surgery as a cure-all for any self-esteem and sexuality woes. In fact, ethical plastic surgeons should screen for this type of behavior and rule out potential patients who may have more serious psychological issues, she said.

"There may be patients who will never be satisfied with their bodies no matter how much surgery they receive or feel that their life will completely change after plastic surgery," Figueroa-Haas said. "These are not ideal candidates for surgery and should seek further counseling to address their underlying psychological issues. But for women who seek improvements in certain physical areas, plastic surgery can be a very positive experience."

Further research should be conducted to assess significant psychosocial issues that may arise after plastic surgery, said Figueroa-Haas, adding that her study helps call attention to the need for health care providers to be able to predict outcomes in this specialized population.

"Since plastic surgery is increasing dramatically, my intention for researching this topic was to evaluate nurses' attitudes toward cosmetic surgery patients and make recommendations for increasing awareness of the factors surrounding these patients," Figueroa-Haas said.

"Nurses should display compassion and understand an individual's reason for seeking cosmetic surgery instead of dismissing or stereotyping these patients." This study shows that there are genuine psychological improvements that follow plastic surgery, and these issues must be understood and respected.

> *"The results are mixed on whether plastic surgery boosts ... self-esteem, quality of life, self-confidence, and interpersonal relationships in the long term."*

# Cosmetic Surgery May Not Improve Self-Esteem

## Melissa Dittmann

*Melissa Dittmann is on the staff of the* Monitor on Psychology, *a publication of the American Psychological Association. In the following viewpoint, the author contends that contradictory findings indicate that cosmetic surgery may not enhance confidence and positive body image in some patients. Very few studies examine the psychological impact of undergoing cosmetic surgery, Dittmann states, and some individuals have mixed results with the outcomes of their procedures or the impact on their personal lives. She advises that psychologists help cosmetic surgeons identify patients who will not adjust well emotionally or mentally after surgery.*

Melissa Dittmann, "Plastic Surgery: Beauty or Beast?" *Monitor on Psychology*, vol. 36, no. 8, September 2005. Copyright © 2005 American Psychological Association. Adapted with permission.

As you read, consider the following questions:

1. As stated by Dittmann, what problems or behaviors may dissatisfied plastic surgery patients show?

2. As written in the viewpoint, how does cosmetic surgery affect those around the recipient?

3. How does cosmetic surgery impact children and adolescents, as described in the viewpoint?

Before the makeover, DeLisa Stiles—a therapist and captain in the Army Reserves—complained of looking too masculine. But on FOX's reality TV makeover show, *The Swan 2*, she morphed into a beauty queen after a slew of plastic surgery procedures—a brow lift, lower eye lift, mid face-lift, fat transfer to her lips and cheek folds, laser treatments for aging skin, tummy tuck, breast lift, liposuction of her inner thighs and dental procedures. The FOX show gives contestants plastic surgery and then has them compete in a beauty pageant, which last year [in 2004] Stiles won.

*The Swan* and other such plastic surgery shows, including ABC's *Extreme Makeover* and MTV's *I Want a Famous Face*, are gaining steam, but some psychologists are concerned about the psychological impact on those who undergo such drastic cosmetic surgery—and also on those who don't and may feel inadequate as a result. While such radical transformations are rare, some psychologists plan to investigate the surge in cosmetic procedures and whether these surgeries have any lasting psychological consequences.

The number of cosmetic procedures increased by 44 percent from 2003 to 2004, according to the American Society for Aesthetic Plastic Surgery. Plastic surgeons conducted a record 11.9 million procedures last year, including nonsurgical procedures like Botox and surgical procedures like breast augmentation or liposuction.

How do such procedures affect patients psychologically? A recent analysis of 37 studies on patients' psychological and psychosocial functioning before and after cosmetic surgery by social worker Roberta Honigman and psychiatrists Katharine Phillips, MD, and David Castle, MD, suggests positive outcomes in patients, including improvements in body image and possibly a quality-of-life boost too. But the same research—published in the April 2004 issue of *Plastic and Reconstructive Surgery*—also found several predictors of poor outcomes, especially for those who hold unrealistic expectations or have a history of depression and anxiety. The researchers found that patients who are dissatisfied with surgery may request repeat procedures or experience depression and adjustment problems, social isolation, family problems, self-destructive behaviors and anger toward the surgeon and his of her staff.

Overall, there are more questions than answers regarding psychological effects of cosmetic surgery: There are few longitudinal studies and many contradictory findings, researchers note. Many studies also contain small sample sizes and short follow-ups with patients, says Castle, a professor and researcher at the Mental Health Research Institute of Victoria in Victoria, Australia.

"We really need good, large prospective studies of representative samples of patients, using well-established research instruments," Castle says. "While most people do well in terms of psychosocial adjustment after such procedures, some do not, and the field needs to be aware of this and to arrange screening for such individuals."

In particular, the extent to which cosmetic surgery affects patients' relationships, self-esteem and quality of life in the long term offers many research opportunities for psychologists, says psychologist Diana Zuckerman, PhD, president of the National Research Center for Women & Families, a think tank that focuses on health and safety issues for women, children and families.

"These are fascinating issues for psychologists to look at—from the cultural phenomena to the interpersonal phenomena to the mental health and self-esteem issues," Zuckerman says.

In addition, plastic surgery issues will increasingly affect clinician psychologists, and the area will offer new roles for them—such as conducting pre- and postsurgical patient assessments, says psychologist David [B.] Sarwer, PhD, director of the [Center for] Weight and Eating Disorders at the University of Pennsylvania. He has studied appearance-related psychological issues, including cosmetic surgery, for the last 10 years.

"As the popularity of plastic surgery continues to grow, many psychologists likely already have—or will encounter—a patient that has thought about or undergone a cosmetic procedure," he says. Therefore it will be increasingly important for psychologists to be able to talk with patients about their appearance concerns and what may make someone a good or bad candidate for cosmetic surgery, he says.

## Research Directions

Equally pressing, however, is the need for research that sheds light on plastic surgery's psychosocial effects, many psychologists agree. To help fill in the gaps, researchers suggest further studies on the following questions:

> *Does plastic surgery make patients feel better?* Studies have shown that people report increased satisfaction with the body part they had surgery on, but results are mixed on whether plastic surgery boosts their self-esteem, quality of life, self-confidence and interpersonal relationships in the long term.

In a recent study, Sarwer—also an associate professor of psychology at the Center for Human Appearance at the University of Pennsylvania School of Medicine—found that a year after receiving cosmetic surgery, 87 percent of patients re-

## Once You Start, It's Hard to Stop

Everyone agrees that once you start, it's hard not to continue. And, of course, what starts with tweaking a bit around the forehead, moves on seamlessly to doing something to those grim lines around the mouth. Then before you know it, there's a simple tuck that could make all the difference to that grim middle-aged mask sneaking up on you.

And it's not only one's peers who are moving the goalpost, but the physically attractive role models we turn to as beacons of possibility, most of whom (particularly our most cherished 'silver stars') have had some kind of help or other.

*Alexandra Shulman, "As Vogue Editor, She's an Arbiter of Beauty*
*—So Why Does Alexandra Shulman Say 'Sorry,*
*But I DEPLORE Cosmetic Surgery?'"*
*Mail Online (UK), May 30, 2008.*

ported satisfaction following their surgery, including improvements in their overall body image and the body feature altered. They also experienced less negative body image emotions in social situations. The study, which was supported by a grant from the Aesthetic Surgery Education and Research Foundation, appeared in the [2005] May/June issue of the *Aesthetic Surgery Journal.* Sarwer and his colleagues plan to follow up with the patients next year.

However, Castle's team found in their literature review—besides some positive outcomes—a link between plastic surgery and poor postsurgical outcomes for some patients, particularly for those with a personality disorder, those who thought the surgery would save a relationship and those who held unrealistic expectations about the procedure.

Some studies have even gone as far as linking dissatisfaction with cosmetic surgery procedures to suicide. For example, in one study, the National Cancer Institute found in 2001 that women with breast implants were four times more likely to commit suicide than other plastic surgery patients of the same age as the women who underwent breast implants, says Zuckerman, who in April [2005] testimony to the Food and Drug Administration (FDA) urged the FDA to deny approval of silicone gel breast implants because of a lack of longitudinal research ensuring their safety.

The other three studies on the topic found the suicide rate to be two to three times greater. Neither of the studies, however, identified a causal relationship between breast implants and suicide. Some researchers speculate that some of the surgery recipients may hold unrealistic expectations of it or have certain personality characteristics that predispose them to suicide.

*How does cosmetic surgery affect those around the recipients?* Physically attractive people often receive preferential treatment and are perceived by others as more sociable, dominant, mentally healthy and intelligent than less attractive people, according to research by psychologist Alan Feingold, PhD, in the March 1992 issue of [American Psychological Association's] APA's *Psychological Bulletin.*

"It's not like looking good doesn't have real advantages—it does," Zuckerman says. "If some people get plastic surgery and other people don't, is that going to put the people who don't at all kinds of disadvantages, such as in finding a job or spouse?"

Nearly 30 years ago, many mental health professionals viewed patients who sought cosmetic surgery as having psychiatric issues, but many studies since then suggest that those who seek cosmetic surgery have few differences pathologically with those who don't have surgery, Sarwer says.

Most people are motivated to undergo cosmetic surgery because of body-image dissatisfaction, says Susan Thorpe, a lecturer in psychology at the University of Surrey in Guildford, Surrey, who conducts cosmetic surgery research.

"They want to look normal—that is, they don't want to stand out in an obvious way or to have features which cause comment or make them feel self-conscious," Thorpe says. "They also want their physical appearance to be more in-line with their personalities and feel that they want all the bits of their bodies to match."

*What effect does plastic surgery have on children and teenagers?* In 2004, about 240,682 cosmetic procedures were performed on patients 18 years old or younger, and the top surgical procedures were nose reshaping, breast lifts, breast augmentation, liposuction and tummy tucks. However, very few studies have been conducted to examine the safety and long-term risks of these procedures on adolescents—an age in which teenagers are still developing mentally and physically, Zuckerman says.

*When does changing your appearance qualify as body dysmorphic disorder (BDD)?* BDD, first introduced in the revised third edition of the *Diagnostic and Statistical Manual of Mental Disorders* in 1987, is characterized by a preoccupation with an aspect of one's appearance. People with BDD repeatedly change or examine the offending body part to the point that the obsession interferes with other aspects of their life. Several studies show that 7 to 12 percent of plastic surgery patients have some form of BDD. Plus, the majority of BDD patients who have cosmetic surgery do not experience improvement in their BDD symptoms, often asking for multiple procedures on the same or other body features.

Sarwer often works with plastic surgeons to help them identify such psychological issues as BDD, so surgeons then can refer patients to mental health professionals. He encourages them to look for the nature of the person's appearance concern, such as whether a patient has an excessive concern with a body feature that appears normal to nearly anyone else. Part of that also includes accounting for patients' internal motivations for surgery—are they doing it for themselves or out of pressure from a romantic partner or friend? And, he encourages surgeons to ensure patients hold realistic expectations about the procedures, rather than expecting the surgery to end long-standing personal issues.

## Psychology's Role

Apart from research, psychologists can find clinical roles in aiding cosmetic surgery patients too, such as helping plastic surgeons conduct such assessments. For example, they can help plastic surgeons identify patients who may not adjust well psychologically or psychosocially after surgery, researchers say.

Castle says that empirically based screening questionnaires will help plastic surgeons select cosmetic surgery patients likely to experience positive psychosocial outcomes.

Sarwer has teamed with other psychologists and plastic surgeons to develop such screening questionnaires, which are included in the book *Psychological Aspects of Reconstructive and Cosmetic Plastic Surgery: Clinical, Empirical and Ethical Perspectives*. The book, to be published this month, features a chapter on how to help both surgeons and mental health professionals screen for BDD, as well as explore the relationships among physical appearance, body image and psychosocial functioning.

Sarwer believes more psychologists will begin to examine issues related to cosmetic surgery because of its increasing popularity and the link between appearance, body image and many psychiatric disorders, such as eating disorders, social phobia and sexual functioning. "Scientifically, we're just starting to catch up to the popularity of [cosmetic surgery] in the population," Sarwer says.

And, as more studies commence, Castle says they need to characterize the population being studied, clearly identify outcome variables and use standardized and state-of-the-art measures.

"There may be strong cultural pressures that are so unrealistic in terms of how we're supposed to look," Zuckerman adds. "Psychologists should . . . figure out why this is happening and what we need to know to make sure that people aren't going to be harmed by this."

> "Women are battling time—and some-
> times winning."

# People Have Cosmetic Surgery to Appear Ageless

*Amy Larocca*

*In the following viewpoint, Amy Larocca claims that cosmetic surgery and anti-aging procedures help women maintain an "ageless" look. She insists that women in their thirties and forties battle wrinkles and other signs of aging with Botox, fillers, lasers, and the surgeon's scalpel, often passing for a decade younger. Nonetheless, Larocca counters that the availability of these treatments creates pressure on women to maintain a youthful appearance and stigmatizes aging. The author is a contributing editor to* New York Magazine *and coauthor of* New York Look Book: A Gallery of Street Fashion.

As you read, consider the following questions:

1. In the author's view, how have the appearances of mothers and daughters changed?
2. What is the biggest reason why women want to remain youthful in appearance, in Larocca's opinion?

Amy Larocca, "The New: Agelessness," *Allure*, vol. 18, no. 4, April 2008, p. 174.

3. According to Terence X. Bogan, why are women in their thirties and forties dressing younger?

Does anyone really look their age anymore? Women are battling time—and sometimes winning.

A couple months ago, my boyfriend came home from a work trip to Los Angeles, walked into our apartment, and made a sudden announcement: "Botox is the new wrinkles," he said.

I knew exactly what he meant. Traditional markers of age—wrinkles, brown spots, that general dullness—have lately ceded to something tight, smooth, expression-free. I've noticed it, too, and not just in Los Angeles. There's a new age out there, and it looks like no age at all. It's a suspended netherworld inhabited by women who might be 28, or 35, or 42, or 50. It's an age we arrived at by way of Botox and fillers—not to mention constant exercise and a new dress code comprised of clothes that at one time would have been considered appropriate only for adolescents. A judicious amount of this stuff can indeed make you look younger, but the trouble is that too much winds up adding years in a "What the hell is she trying to hide?" way. Old-fashioned wrinkles can be far less damning than desperate attempts at patching them up.

Sometimes I find myself strolling on a sidewalk behind two girls with matching perky butts in skinny designer jeans and that lush, highlighted, Gisele-esque hair. I assume the girls are classmates (and best friends/mean girls) at some very fancy high school, only to realize on closer inspection that they are actually mother and daughter. They don't look alike exactly, but they are no longer different in the ways that mothers and daughters have historically been different: The daughters often are the ones who look far more sophisticated and groomed, while their mothers look, frankly, kind of confused.

Name a sign of aging, and a dermatologist can likely proffer a fix. Tired eyes? Shoot a little filler underneath. Crow's-feet? Inject just a bit of Botox. Spotty skin? Expanding pores? Zap them with lasers. "There's a ten-year—or more—standard deviation when it comes to aging these days," says Jeannette Graf, a Great Neck, New York, dermatologist who specializes in anti-aging treatments. "If someone does all of these treatments, she can take 10 to 15 years off. When someone is 40, there's no reason she can't pass for 30—or even younger. It's an ageless look." Graf points out that she and other dermatologists aren't aiming to change patients' essential features—just to turn back, and then, fingers crossed, stop the clock.

But even when these treatments are done well, they may still have one major ramification. Stopping the clock for some can seem to speed it up for others: After all, the younger your peers look, the older you do. And in this way, these treatments are driving a more widespread preoccupation with appearing as youthful as possible. Women are feeling increasing pressure not just to look good for their age, but to actually never age at all. As Phyllis R. Koch-Sheras, a Charlottesville, Virginia, clinical psychologist who has studied the effect of aging on women, puts it: "We tend to have much more help denying aging than we do accepting it."

## Younger Inside

In college, and during those delirious years after, I considered aging to be something weird that happened to other people—"a rumor," as [British author] Martin Amis famously put it. I'd always figured that when the time came (which, if I'm being completely honest, I never thought it would), I'd slip gracefully into gentle white hair and a kind, lined face. I imagined, from the poreless perspective of 23, that softening hips and sagging skin would feel like the emblems of a sage-like wisdom I hoped to gain. I felt pity for women who couldn't accept nature, and thought the mad scramble to arrest time was embarrassing and sad.

But then 30 arrived, and evening cocktails started causing morning bags beneath my eyes. Ancient sunburns came back to haunt me in the form of blotches and dark spots. Panic set in. "But I am still young!" I wanted to shout to the mirror. "Wait!"

I guess, if I'm being honest, the panic comes from feeling that I don't deserve the little crow's-feet that have begun to work their way toward my temples. There's still so much to do, see, live. "We feel younger inside than we look," says Leslie Baumann, a Miami dermatologist who starts many of her patients on Botox at age 25. "It can be disturbing." She's right. A recent survey from the Boomer Project, a market research and consulting firm, found that on average, female baby boomers feel 12 years younger than their chronological age.

Despite the fact that in our minds, most of us feel like we're barely adults, the biggest reason why I think women of my generation are so intent on looking young is simply that we can afford it. We earn much more of our own disposable income than our mothers and grandmothers did, and are free to spend it on vanity in a way women never were before. The treatments exist, and we have the money to pay for them.

I often wonder whether our fitness-crazed culture also has something to do with our generation's collective horror at getting older. My mother and grandmother have always maintained their slim figures with strict diets and light exercise, like walking in the afternoons. I don't think either of them has done a sit-up in her life. I, and all of my friends, huff and puff and lunge and squat in a sweaty attempt not to defy aging exactly, just to delay it a drop.

"Forty for us was 30 for other generations," my trainer, David Kirsch, owner of the Madison Square Club in New York City, tells me one morning when I ask (while performing a spastic set of high kicks with weighted bands Velcroed to my legs) if I should expect my butt to age differently than my mom's. "It's going to be a whole different thing," he says. Ro-

byn M. Stuhr, an exercise physiologist and the executive vice president of the American Council on Exercise, says that working out often can indeed keep your body looking young. "The research clearly shows that regular exercise can prevent loss of muscle, bone, mobility, strength, and stamina—and keep excess fat from creeping on, particularly around the abdominal area," she says. "All of those effects are associated with youth." Plus, it may make you just seem younger. "It can boost your self-esteem, physical function, and energy while decreasing any anxiety and depression," says Stuhr, "which can lead to having a positive and vibrant outlook on life that tends to come across as more youthful."

## Outrunning Time

I do think that all the running and Spinning and yoga and Pilates and Yogalates we're up to all the time is having a psychological effect to match its physiological one. If we can keep our bodies supple, shouldn't our faces—and lifestyles, and mentality—match?

And as bodies become toned, rather than merely slim, women have stopped wearing modest, "age-appropriate" post-30 clothes. Terence X. Bogan, a vice president at Barneys New York who is responsible for the store's Co-Op division, where jeans are sold, says his customers are getting older and older. "At the inception of Co-Op more than 15 years ago, we thought our customer would skew young," he says. That idea is, increasingly, wrong. "We've started seeing skinny jeans on women of all ages," he says. "Bell-bottoms, minidresses, things that are very body conscious. Our thirty- and fortysomething customers work really hard on their bodies; they pay a lot for their bodies at the gym—and in the plastic surgeon's operating room—and they want to show them off."

And we have the sheer time to spend in the gym, in the store, in the dermatologist's office—to, in short, be consumed by vanity—because so many of us are delaying getting married and having kids. The absence of that kind of responsibility also leads to a younger mind-set. By 32 (my age now), my mother and grandmother had both married and had (multiple!) kids. They lived in real houses, where the refrigerators were always stocked with orange juice and leafy greens. They had such mature lives that accepting a maturing body and face must've seemed like it was part of the deal.

I trudge up four flights to the one-bedroom apartment I share with my boyfriend, and perhaps because we do our dishes by hand (or, too often, don't), sleep too late, and are almost always out of milk, I feel like I should look young enough for such a laid-back setup. A life marked by so few real responsibilities should have a worry- and crease-free complexion to match, right? Or do I keep up the lifestyle because bounding up those four flights is easier now than it would've been for someone who'd never been to a gym? Koch-Sheras sees the delayed maturation as an attempt to postpone aging and points out that you can't put it off indefinitely: "Time does catch up with you eventually." Doesn't mean we can't try to outrun it, though.

But it's not only single women who are resisting age: Women who marry and have children when they're young are taking cues from their untethered counterparts and are becoming serious time-fighters, too—moving directly from the maternity ward to boob lifts and tummy tucks. Plastic surgeons now offer special postpartum packages to the new moms stunned by pictures of Heidi Klum modeling lingerie weeks after giving birth or Gwyneth Paltrow's board-flat abs, made to feel that even motherhood is no longer a valid reason for, well, looking like a mother.

## The Botox No-Age

Which brings us to this: Despite the books and TV shows glorifying stunning fortyish singletons . . . it's not all shopping sprees and Botox parties. Despite the fact that we've had things pretty easy compared to women who've come before us, all the opportunities we have create very high expectations for us. And let's face it: We're entitled. We're the first generation who grew up not just thinking we could be, but expecting to be, a famous fashion designer, an astronaut, a brain surgeon, or the president of the United States—all the while looking gorgeous and staying eternally youthful. We're accustomed to getting our way. But the fight against aging, while not impossible to win, is a serious adversary—and that is unnerving to us.

A few weeks ago I went to a screening of an independent film and then on to a dinner party. At the coat check, I was chatting with a friend when a (much older) man butted his head between us and asked, point-blank, without a softening introduction, how old I was.

I'm embarrassed to report that I instantly got completely, outrageously defensive. I felt angry that he would make me reveal my age in front of others, even my friends. "What?" I shouted, far louder than was necessary. "What's the matter with you?" I called him "creepy and rude," turned huffy and crimson, and was eventually calmed down by his mortified wife. "We have a daughter," she reasonably explained. "We were wondering if she'd like the film." Oh. Never mind.

Over dinner, my friends and I discussed why I'd gotten so upset. Everyone—male and female—agreed that "What do you earn in a year?" would've been a similarly rude and presumptive query. The man was not evil. Socially awkward, yes, but not evil.

For days afterward, I winced when I thought about my dramatic response. I kept replaying it in my mind. Why couldn't I have just smiled, answered proudly, and calmly questioned why he asked? I hated the idea of being ashamed of my age; I hated that I was suddenly hoping to conceal it, to enter into that liminal Botox no-age.

So far there have been no needles, no knives, no pulsing beams of infrared light aimed at my face. I take what I consider to be reasonable precautions: I try, when I can resist it, to stay out of the sun, and my medicine cabinet is like a clown car of creams. I still like to think that I won't make clock-stopping a top priority in my adult life, but I no longer feel critical of women who do. And I no longer declare that I never will. But if I ever do, I hope I'll keep my objectives in check, because when it comes to 25—been there, done that. Why in the world should I try to do it again?

> *"Could it be that the quest for wrinkle-free perfection soon may be coming to an end?"*

# People Who Have Cosmetic Surgery Want to Look Good for Their Age

*Wendy Lewis*

*In the following viewpoint, Wendy Lewis suggests that individuals who have plastic surgery and cosmetic treatments desire to look their best, not younger or physically flawless. She contends that attitudes about looks and aging are shifting: Women want to appear refreshed and look their age, not unnatural and artificially free of wrinkles. Along with healthy diets and exercise, breakthrough injectable treatments such as Botox and fillers are a part of the beauty routine for an increasing number of people, she states. Lewis is an image-enhancement coach and author of* Plastic Makes Perfect: The Complete Cosmetic Beauty Guide *and other beauty books.*

As you read, consider the following questions:

1. How do Americans differ in their beauty treatments and routines than Europeans, in Lewis's view?

Wendy Lewis, "The Changing Face of Beauty," *USA Today*, vol. 138, no. 2774, November 2009, p. 64–66. Copyright © 2009 Society for the Advancement of Education. Reproduced by permission.

2. What is the "era of glamour," according to Sander Gilman?

3. In her opinion, why have Lewis's clients changed from women who want to look younger to an atypical group?

When it comes to beauty perceptions—and habits—there long has been a great cultural divide. Yet, with the globalization of the media, one wonders how these cultural differences affect what is considered beautiful, whether all women strive for the same beauty goals, and if there is one universal image that ranks the highest across cultures.

According to an international study of men and women's beauty perceptions and grooming routines, women want to look good for their age—not necessarily younger. Whether you hail from Los Angeles, London, or Lyon [France], these findings suggest an important trend in the perception of beauty and attractiveness. We are witnessing a backlash to the era of the extreme, tightly pulled, over-enhanced look. Could it be that the quest for wrinkle-free perfection soon may be coming to an end?

Sander Gilman, a medical and cultural historian from Emory University, speaking about Aesthetic Anthropology—which examines the cultural differences in beauty and grooming perceptions and habits—explains that there is no single standard of attractiveness across cultures and the image of beauty has changed over time and throughout the world. Yet, all countries share some similarities. One constant is that balance and symmetry, radiant skin, and full contours are considered beautiful. Since the dawn of history, human beings have been looking for ways to slow or halt the aging process. Our dissatisfaction with our looks motivates an entire list of behaviors, including losing weight as well as employing moisturizer, hair dye, and nonsurgical injectable products—and, in some cases, having surgery. The desire to improve one's self is a natural consequence of living in an image-conscious society.

Ultimately, cosmetic enhancements offer what many cultures value most: aesthetic improvement and the preservation of youthfulness and vitality.

According to Gilman, we have entered an "Era of Glamour," in which it is accessible and publicly accepted for everyone—from Hollywood's A-list to the Midwestern soccer mom—to look glamorous, but perhaps not in the usual sense of the term. Gilman notes the Era of Glamour started with the Botox Cosmetic Revolution, during which nonsurgical options to diminish facial lines became accessible, affordable, and provided a natural, relaxed look without the long recovery time of cosmetic surgery. According to the American Society for Aesthetic Plastic Surgery (ASAPS), in the handful of years since receiving approval from the Food and Drug Administration, Botox Cosmetic treatments have increased 238%. Last year [2008] alone, more than 3,000,000 treatments took place.

To examine the implications of our culture on beauty routines and perceptions, Allergan, Inc., the maker of Botox Cosmetic (botulinum toxin type A) and the Juvéderm family of dermal fillers, surveyed more than 10,000 women and men from the U.S., United Kingdom, Italy, Spain, France, and Germany to identify their attitudes toward beauty and grooming. The "Aesthetic Anthropology Survey of Beauty and Grooming Across Cultures" found U.S. women are significantly less wrinkle tolerant than Europeans. This is exactly what I find with my clients: Americans are more proactive about looking after themselves and more willing to make the investment long term. They embark on beauty treatments earlier, often in their 20s and 30s, as preventative measures, while European women tend to start in their 40s and 50s with an emphasis on correction and restoration. In my experience, Americans are more demanding about the return they get from their beauty treatments. They seek out science-based products, have higher expectations for products they use, and often follow the advice of beauty professionals. If something does not work, Americans will switch or trade up. In contrast, European women often use the same skin care and cosmetics handed down to them from their mothers and grandmothers.

American women are much more likely to report feeling like they look stressed and tired. This probably is because they are. Europeans enjoy four weeks of vacation, whereas a large number of Americans take a one-week vacation during the summer. Europeans long have enjoyed their lives in a more traditional way by taking time away from the office for naps, family events, and to pursue relaxation as a lifestyle. The survey found European women are less age-obsessed than Americans are. They do not mind their lines and creases nearly as much. I have found my European clients to be "cautious followers" who are more traditional in their beauty routines.

Anthropologist Isabella Lepri, a researcher from the London School of Economics [and Political Science], elaborates on the universal emphasis the human race has on appearance. "People everywhere have always endeavored to look attractive for many reasons. However, what is beautiful varies tremendously and, in the Western world, we are currently seeing a shift. There is an ever-growing pressure on people, especially women, to be successful as well as to look good, which constantly challenges their self-esteem."

The survey results suggest that the pendulum is swinging from an overwhelming desire to look younger toward an attitude of making the most of what you have. "Today," says Lepri, "the ultimate challenge is to meet all the expectations while looking effortlessly, naturally beautiful, but feeling good about yourself, taking pride in your accomplishments. In fact, liking what you see in the mirror may no longer be defined by the need to look perfect."

Also of interest is that, based on Gilman's experience, men (not women) are the catalyst for the growing acceptance of nonsurgical aesthetic treatments. Way back in the 1890s, men underwent the majority of surgical procedures, often claiming to repair a deviated septum—and thus categorizing the procedures as "medical." In the 1900s, there was a cultural shift and women began undergoing the same surgery. However, at this time, the procedure commonly became known as a "nose job," a cosmetic procedure steeped in vanity.

We are at another crux of change based on men's influence. Following the metrosexual trend of the 1990s during which it became socially acceptable for men to invest in their grooming routines, according to ASAPS, men's use of nonsurgical aesthetic treatments spiked. "Following men's acceptance of aesthetic treatments to diminish wrinkles," explains Gilman, "there has been a shift in the public's attitude about looking attractive from one of 'vanity' to one of 'health.'"

Boomers now glide into their twilight years like no other generation before. They are living longer and medical science has given them the tools to impact the aging process in terms of diagnostics, medicines, nutrition, and cosmetic procedures. In my practice, I see men and women who personally have redefined the concept of aging. While aging is inevitable, they have decided to manage the process. They choose healthy lifestyles, eat balanced diets, work out regularly, take vitamins, and have accepted that nonsurgical treatments now are part of this routine to look their very best.

## Living Wrinkle Free

The Aesthetic Anthropology survey found that, while 80% of women across the U.S. and Europe recognize they have wrinkles or fine lines, some 44% would like to get rid of all of their wrinkles. It seems apparent that dermal fillers and wrinkle relaxers play a major role in shaping the changing face of 21st-century beauty. After ophthalmologists began using botulinum toxin type A to treat eye conditions in the late 1980s, they quickly discovered an added benefit—a softening of the wrinkles around the eyes. In 2002 the Food and Drug

Administration [FDA] approved Botox Cosmetic for the temporary improvement in the appearance of moderate to severe glabellar lines (the vertical "frown lines" between the brows which often appear as an "||"). ASAPS data indicates that Botox is the number one aesthetic treatment in the U.S.

Since the 1880s, physicians have been developing ways to restore volume and structure to aging skin using a variety of approaches, including paraffin, silicone, and collagen injections. The earliest substances used for plumping facial wrinkles had a number of side effects. Fat injections were used as early as the late 19th century, although rather unsuccessfully. It was difficult to control where the fat could be placed, and it tended to migrate and become absorbed quickly, so the cherubic look faded quickly.

Gilman shares the tale of Consuelo Vanderbilt, "who in the 1960s was considered the most beautiful woman in the world. At a certain age, she treated her facial wrinkles with paraffin injections. As the paraffin began to shift, she formed unsightly scars and became disfigured causing her to become a recluse for the last decades of her life."

Europeans have had a wider selection of dermal fillers and wrinkle-relaxing injections available, due to a less stringent regulatory environment. Only recently has the FDA started approving multiple demand filler options. Today, ASAPS statistics show that hyaluronic acid-base dermal fillers, such as Juvéderm, are the fastest-growing nonsurgical aesthetic procedures in the U.S. The most common areas treated with dermal fillers are the parentheses running from the sides of the bottom of the nose to the outer corners of the mouth. Most often, Botox Cosmetic is used to relax the underlying muscles in the upper-third of the face, while fillers treat the lower portion.

When I started my consultancy in 1997, my typical client almost exclusively was a female in her 40s—or older. Overwhelmingly, these women were seeking age-reversing surgery, including face and brow lifts and eyelid procedures. Today, there is no typical client, reflecting the shifting dynamics of the global aesthetics industry as a whole. This pattern is a function of several developments including the proliferation of safe, effective, and affordable nonsurgical and minimally invasive procedures; the erosion of the stigma surrounding having a little "work" done; and the explosion of information available to consumers seeking cosmetic enhancements.

While the Aesthetic Anthropology survey uncovered only a small percentage of Americans and Europeans undergoing injectable treatments at present, it also found that 40% of U.S. and European women state they would consider injectables. In the U.S. today, there are more than 6,000 board certified plastic surgeons and over 10,000 dermatologists. Many more health care professionals across medical specialties also are offering aesthetic enhancements in the form of injectables, skin care treatments, and laser procedures to meet growing consumer demand. In my role as an image-enhancement coach, I tell my clients to be careful and to seek out only FDA-approved products from a trained and qualified medical professional.

In the survey, one-third of all women revealed that their beauty routine has a more significant impact on their self-esteem than it did five years ago, and about half of women are satisfied with their beauty and grooming practices. As long as we have wrinkles, there will be a market for everything anti-aging. Cosmetic treatments are on the upswing, and the numbers reflect the growing acceptance of image enhancements among women and men.

We are witnessing a sea of change in global attitude towards the process of cosmetic enhancement. Women no longer want an extreme makeover, rather they want to look refreshed and relaxed—like themselves, but better. We are coming to realize that absolute perfection neither is realistic nor attainable, but looking healthy, radiant, and good for your age definitely is achievable.

*"Cosmetic surgery is being deployed
as a deliberate instrument of career
advancement."*

# People Have Cosmetic Surgery to Make More Money

*Liz Wolgemuth*

*In the following viewpoint, Liz Wolgemuth says that many
Americans undergo cosmetic surgery in a bid to increase their
salaries and advance their careers. In particular, procedures such
as hair transplants and eyelid surgery are spreading among men
in the corporate world, she maintains. Furthermore, evidence
suggests that looking good pays off, asserts Wolgemuth: Beauty
and youth are associated with traits such as intelligence and
power, and attractive employees are more likely to receive raises,
promotions, and preferential treatment than their plainer counterparts are. Wolgemuth reports on careers and employment for
U.S. News & World Report.*

As you read, consider the following questions:

1. How does Wolgemuth support her claim that more
   women and men seek plastic surgery to remain competitive in the workplace?

Liz Wolgemuth, "Nip and Tuck for More Bucks," *U.S. News & World Report*, vol. 144,
no. 18, June 23, 2008, p. 68. Copyright © 2008 U.S. News & World Report, L.P.
Reprinted with permission.

2. What does Gordon Patzer predict about cosmetic surgery?

3. What is Judy Jernudd's position on cosmetic surgery for career advancement?

Unless you're [model] Heidi Klum or [soccer player] David Beckham, you probably don't want to hear the research about physical appearance and its not-so-subtle effect on your career: Good looks may influence the salary you earn and the opportunities you have for advancement.

But more and more Americans are facing the, well, ugly news head-on. They're opting to nip, tuck, or transplant their way to a better job or a bigger paycheck. Indeed, far from the glare of the Hollywood klieg lights—where God-given is generally long-gone—cosmetic surgery is being deployed as a deliberate instrument of career advancement.

The American Academy of Facial Plastic and Reconstructive Surgery reports that last year [in 2007] about two-thirds of its members reported seeing men and women who requested cosmetic surgery because they wanted to remain competitive in the workplace. In his nine years of practice, Antonio Armani, a Beverly Hills, Calif., cosmetic surgeon who specializes in hair transplants, says there's been a growing desire among corporate men—often working in finance—to look younger.

But as a career investment, a youthful hairline doesn't come cheap. Armani says a typical transplant procedure costs from $15,000 to $35,000. While his patients often are wealthy, many younger men are financing the cost. Recently, a marine coming off active duty took out a $25,000 loan for his surgery, Armani says, because he "wants to look good" as he heads into law school. While women used to bear the bulk of society's aesthetic pressures, men now feel that their looks have equal bearing on their success. In the corporate world, "people really feel that if they look better, they will do better, they will get the job they were competing for," Armani says.

## The Advantages of Looking Good

Cringe-worthy or not, there's research to back up that claim. Gordon [L.] Patzer, author of *Looks: Why They Matter More than You Ever Imagined* and a longtime researcher on the impact of physical attractiveness, can run through a laundry list of study results that point to the advantages of looking good. Cuter newborns in a nursery are touched, held, and talked to more than less attractive babies. Schoolteachers unknowingly tend to hold higher expectations for better-looking children. Parents may be less protective of less attractive children.

Then, when people reach working age, good-looking college graduates are more likely to get hired. Employees themselves tend to be willing to do more for better-looking bosses. Attractive supervisors are perceived as more credible and more persuasive.

When James Gould, an ear, nose, and throat doctor in St. Louis, began losing his hair in his mid-thirties, he did what most men do. He tried to cover it up—growing it a bit longer than usual and dyeing it to conceal the thinning patches. But it backfired: An employee gave her thumbs down to the dye job, and a patient told him: "You can afford to do something about it."

Gould, 41, underwent a hair transplant in an effort to get back the youthful, confident appearance he felt he'd begun to lose—an appearance he felt was important to his job. "I think patients to some degree kind of look up to their physicians to be little more than human," Gould says. "To have your hair suddenly falling out in patches, it kind of looks like there's something wrong with your health."

Certain cosmetic procedures may offer the most bang for your buck. Men have been turning to eyelid surgery. It was the fourth most common surgical cosmetic procedure last year, and the second most popular among men, according to the American Society of Plastic Surgeons. Also, teeth whitening is a great investment, because teeth turn gray as we age, Patzer says.

Patzer does not particularly enjoy the results of his research. With society putting far too much emphasis on physical attractiveness and the bias in favor of good looks being so widespread and discriminatory, he often says that "beauty can be ugly." But he doesn't believe there will be a change in our preference for physically attractive people any time soon. Attitudes, social norms, and technological advances are going to make cosmetic surgery increasingly common, Patzer says. He predicts it will become a tool in career advancement—just like clothes or education.

Penelope Trunk, a careers blogger and author of *Brazen Careerist*, predicted in a blog entry earlier this year that plastic surgery will become a tool "for the go-getters and career-minded" and will even be a routine procedure for college grads.

Judy Jernudd, an executive coach, helps her corporate clients improve their body language, appearance, and clothing, often using a video camera to show a slumped posture or unenthusiastic delivery. She thinks surgery should be used sparingly. But in the end, if that's what it takes, so be it. "I'm not encouraging everyone to go out and get cosmetic surgery," Jernudd says. "I think there are people that can go overboard on cosmetic surgery. But I do think that you can see people—if it's done correctly—where they can look 10 years younger."

Hollywood has long relied on the skill of the scalpel to preserve—or jump-start—careers. But Main Street seems to be feeling the same competitive pressures. Denise Thomas, a New York cosmetic surgery consultant, says working women who begin to see their younger colleagues score job promotions seek cosmetic surgery to get a second shot at workplace success. "It says on my Web site: 'Youth and beauty are power tools,'" Thomas says. "People equate youth with power and money."

History is, of course, full of very successful individuals who weren't much to look at: Think Napoleon or Albert Einstein. But these are the exceptions, and they don't disprove the rule, Patzer says. Who knows, if Einstein would've had a little work done—or at least dragged a comb through that tangle of hair—he might have won two Nobel Prizes.

## Looking Good—For a Price

Here are four cosmetic procedures that experts say might offer the best career boost for the buck. (Prices noted are averages for physicians' fees only.)

- Eyelid surgery ($3,134): Why go for an eyelid pick-me-up? Perceptions of youth and health correlate with physical attractiveness. This is a popular pick for men.

- Face-lift ($5,031): Face-lifts are a classic among older women, possibly because they can boost confidence, which, in itself, offers a big career payoff.

- Rhinoplasty ($3,833): A well-done nose job has, for some patients, fixed a feature that hindered a strong self-image. Popular among all age groups.

- Teeth whitening: A cheap but effective way ($30 from pharmacy, $600 at the dentist) to look more youthful.

# Periodical Bibliography

*The following articles have been selected to supplement the diverse views presented in this chapter.*

| | |
|---|---|
| Guy Adams | "Alicia Douvall: Addicted to Cosmetic Surgery," *Independent* (London), February 10, 2009. |
| Allison Adato | "Obsessed with Plastic Surgery," *People*, January 15, 2007. |
| CBS News | "Cosmetic Surgery Can Boost Mood," October 9, 2006. |
| Marilyn W. Edmunds and Laurie Scudder | "The Portrayal of Cosmetic Surgery in Popular Magazines," *Medscape Today*, February 3, 2009. |
| Marie Murray | "Who Is the Plastic-est of Them All?" *Irish Times*, September 24, 2005. |
| Madison Park | "Celeb Lookalike Surgery Requests Raise Red Flags," CNN.com, July 27, 2010. www.cnn.com. |
| Beth Spencer | "Are Wrinkles Really All That Ugly?" *Age*, October 27, 2006. |
| Camille Sweeney | "Seeking Self-Esteem Through Surgery," *New York Times*, January 14, 2009. |
| Susan Todd | "Older Job-Seekers Find Plastic Surgery Gives Them an Edge," *Star-Ledger* (New Jersey), May 10, 2009. |
| Molly F. Wetterschneider | "Unpeeling Cosmetic Surgery's Glossy Surface," SciTini, September 19, 2006. www.bu.edu. |

OPPOSING
VIEWPOINTS®
SERIES

CHAPTER 4

# What Is the Future of Cosmetic Surgery?

# Chapter Preface

In 2004, Connie Culp, an Ohio woman in her mid-forties, was shot in the face by her husband. The blast obliterated her nose, one eye, cheekbone, upper jaw, and, essentially, the basic facial structure of bone, muscle, and skin. Despite thirty operations, reconstructive surgeons could not restore her ability to breathe normally (she had a tube inserted in her neck) and eat solid food, nor could they relieve the pain caused by scarring. Furthermore, Culp could no longer live a normal life, feared as a "monster" by children and gawked at by strangers.

Four years later, Culp received the first face transplant in the nation, allowing her to breathe and eat normally once again. "You appreciate the little things that you didn't realize before,"[1] Culp said in a video on the *Oprah Winfrey Show* a year later. Plastic surgeon Maria Siemionow, who led Culp's transplant, believes it gives hope to survivors of disfiguring and catastrophic injuries. "There are so many patients in their houses where they are hiding from society, because they are afraid to go to the grocery store, afraid to walk the streets,"[2] Siemionow asserts. "We hope that this special group of patients will one day be able to go comfortably from their houses."

Another plastic surgeon, Simon Whitney contends that, in the future, face transplants may eventually shape tomorrow's cosmetic surgery. "We've seen how an ear can be grown on the back of a mouse,"[3] Whitney observes. "That has been done. We may be able to grow an entire new face in the lab from our own tissue samples. That is not inconceivable." In fact, many cosmetic procedures such as rhinoplasty have been

1. Oprah.com, "Inside Connie's Life Video," September 21, 2009. www.oprah.com.

2. MedicineNet.com, "Surgeons Describe 1st U.S. Face Transplant," May 6, 2009. www .medicinenet.com.

3. Josh Sims, "Face Transplant," *Sabotage Times*, May 7, 2010. www.sabotagetimes.com.

applied first in reconstructive manners. Therefore, the prospect of face transplantation disturbs some critics who fear the procedure may evolve from reconstructive to purely aesthetic purposes. Citing the case of a hand transplant recipient who ultimately had the appendage removed, British writer Josh Sims argues that "with the face the outward seat of our identity, the psychological impact is so much the greater: Can we relate to ourselves, or can others relate to us in the same way, with another face?"[4] In the following chapter, the authors look to the future of cosmetic surgery.

4. Ibid.

| "Taxing elective cosmetic surgery is a great way to raise revenue for health care reform."

# Cosmetic Surgery Should Be Taxed

### Part I: Jessica Dweck, Part II: Claudia Deutsch

*In the following viewpoints, the authors defend the proposed 5 percent tax on cosmetic surgery, which was ultimately omitted from the 2010 U.S. health care bill. In Part I, Jessica Dweck puts forward that the tax would discourage risky elective surgeries and create revenue for the universal health care overhaul. In Part II, Claudia Deutsch dismisses the argument that the tax is sexist toward women, who make up the majority of cosmetic surgery patients. Instead, she insists that if Botox injections and other procedures cost more, the pressure on women to look young would diminish. Dweck is an intern at DoubleX, a Web magazine for women. A former business reporter for the* New York Times, *Deutsch writes the Bottom Line column at True/Slant, an online news network.*

Part I: Jessica Dweck, "In Defense of the Nip/Tax," *DoubleX*, November 24, 2009. Reproduced by permission of Slate. Part II: Claudia Deutsch, "Tax Facelifts—and Strike a Blow Against Ageism," True/Slant, November 30, 2009. Reproduced by permission.

As you read, consider the following questions:

1. For what three reasons does Dweck oppose a tax on cosmetic surgery?
2. How does Deutsch definite a "vanity tax"?
3. How does society treat aging differently for men and women, according to Deutsch?

With all due respect to *Slate*'s Christopher Beam, I don't agree that the "botax" tucked into the Senate health care bill is a bad idea. Much as it pains me to swallow conventional wisdom, the obvious conclusion in this case—that taxing elective cosmetic surgery is a great way to raise revenue for health care reform—also happens to be the correct one.

## Three Dimensions

Tax-policy buffs generally analyze taxes along three dimensions: equity, efficiency, and economic stabilization. Beam goes for the triad, arguing, first, that a tax on elective plastic surgery would unfairly penalize the lower-middle-income consumers who make up the bulk of the market. (Though, with the prevalence of cosmetic procedures among teens and young adults whose parents foot the bill, I question the persuasiveness of his statistic that one-third of plastic surgery consumers earn less than $30,000.) Second, the tax would harm the cosmetic surgery industry and dampen its stimulating effect on the economy. Third, due to the hazy boundary between "reconstructive" and "elective" plastic surgery, high administrative costs would render its enforcement economically inefficient.

These points would be valid for an income or payroll tax. They are almost entirely irrelevant when scrutinizing a sumptuary, or "sin" tax, which is what this one is. The point isn't to make wealthier people pay more. It's to discourage some morally questionable or socially harmful behavior. Cigarettes are the paradigmatic example.

One could also argue that the surprisingly paltry average income among plastic surgery recipients actually presents a more potent argument for the botax. This is one instance of paternalism where father [Barack] Obama knows best. If the majority of those going under the knife cannot afford to do so, the government should dissuade its low-earning citizens from frittering away their scarce resources on larger breasts and firmer calves and encourage them to invest in education instead.

The Senate is proposing a tax on elective cosmetic surgery. And—what a shock—plastic surgeons are outraged. [According to NYTimes.com]:

> The proposal—called the Bo-Tax, in a play on the name of Botox, the popular wrinkle-eliminating treatment—has outraged plastic surgeons, who say they are being singled out because of an outdated perception that people who have cosmetic procedures are well-to-do. . . .
>
> The 7,000-member American Society of Plastic Surgeons said its internal surveys showed that 60 percent of members' patients earn less than $90,000 a year.

Okay, let's not even touch how ludicrous it is to use $90,000 as the level below which poverty kicks in. I simply don't get the objections to the tax at all. Appendectomies are medically necessary; face-lifts are not. You don't pay tax on aspirin, you do on rouge. So what? This is a vanity tax, pure and simple, and thus falls into the same category as sin taxes—if you want to indulge in risky or silly behavior, fine, but it'll cost you.

## Perpetrating Ageism

But I am particularly outraged by another argument being made against this tax: That it discriminates against women, who certainly get nipped and tucked and injected more than men. The question, of course, is why do they? And we all know the answer.

Society has persuaded us that aging men look distinguished, aging women look decrepit, that lined male faces are craggy, lined female faces are wrinkled, that men gain more authority as they age, while women are taken ever less seriously. And by getting the injections, the operations, all those things, we let them perpetuate the tyranny.

I was at a close friend's home for dinner Friday night. At one point her young son asked how old I was. Before I could answer, she hushed him up—"That's an impolite question, we don't ask it." Why not? I asked. It's none of his business, she said. If he asked me how tall I am, or where I live, would that be none of his business also? I asked. No, she said, but it's just that he's so much younger than you. Yes he is, said I—but why should this somehow make me embarrassed about my age? He's also shorter than me. I turned to the young man and very loudly announced my age. Simultaneously one of his teenaged sisters said, "Good for you!" while another one said, "Oh, great, you've now made it harder for other women." (For the record, June 11, 1947, do the math—but now you have to send me a birthday present.)

I don't get it. Do I wish I were younger? You betcha. I also wish I were taller. And richer. And I wish I had much thicker hair. Doesn't mean I'm gonna lie about my height, or live beyond my means, or invest in hair extensions. Why in tarnation should I lie about my age, or take drastic measures to hide it?

Sure, I want to look good. And when someone tells me I look younger, I get the sense they are telling me I look healthy, maybe even pretty. And sure, I use makeup. And I won't swear that I won't get Botoxed or Juvédermed or even lifted.

But right now, I'm too darned angry at a society that thinks I'm silly NOT to do those things. So, coming full circle on this argument, I would love to see a tax that would (1) raise needed money to insure poor people, and (2) maybe, just maybe, restore some dignity to healthy aging.

*"Ultimately, the cosmetic tax is not an effective fund-raising scheme that affects only the privileged few who live on Fifth Avenue and shop on Rodeo Drive."*

# Cosmetic Surgery Should Not Be Taxed

*Haideh Hirmand*

*Haideh Hirmand is a plastic surgeon at New York-Presbyterian Hospital and clinical assistant professor of surgery at Weill Cornell Medical College. In the following viewpoint, Hirmand opposes the planned 5 percent tax on cosmetic surgery, which was ultimately omitted from the 2010 U.S. health care bill. The author argues the tax would discriminate against women, who are the vast majority of cosmetic surgery recipients; compel patients to seek unsafe procedures performed by unqualified personnel; and make it difficult in determining which procedures are cosmetic or reconstructive. Support for the tax, Hirmand concludes, is driven by the misperception that cosmetic surgery is a privilege of the affluent.*

Haideh Hirmand, "The Real Cost of a 'Botax,'" Women on the Web, December 8, 2009. Reproduced by permission.

As you read, consider the following questions:

1. In the author's view, why would the cosmetic surgery tax cost the middle class?

2. How does Hirmand support the claim that the state tax on cosmetic surgery in New Jersey is a failure?

3. How would the tax violate patient privacy, as stated by Hirmand?

Thinking about a touch of Botox before your next event? Perhaps a little filler before your next job interview? Or even some liposuction now that menopause has hit and no matter what you do, you're carrying a little extra plumpness around the middle? You may want to move fast or consider a trip abroad or even start researching non-licensed practitioners who can perform these procedures. Sounds ridiculous, doesn't it?

When I first heard about the 5% tax on elective procedures that is being proposed in the Senate health [care] reform bill, there was a moment of "wow"—and then I paused to reflect. The "wow" came because there was intuitively something arbitrary and bizarre about the tax, which came out of left field. Why the pause? I am not part of the knee-jerk opposition that immediately balks at anything from the Right or the Left. After all, as physicians we understand the need and value of health care reform that actually improves access to and quality of care. I also understand the fiscal constraints of these times and the need to limit expanding the deficit.

So last week [December 2009], one of my out-of-state patients sheepishly observed—with the kind of guilt that often accompanies cosmetic surgery—that the proposed "Bo-tax," the first federal tax of its kind, would probably not make a big difference for my patients. Inspired, I set out to do my own research. I knew that next door in New Jersey there was a similar state tax in place, so at least we had a small model to look at. The more I learned, the more outrage I felt. Here's what I found out.

## Discrimination Against Women

*The tax discriminates against women:* According to the American Society for Aesthetic Plastic Surgery (ASAPS), 91% of all cosmetic procedures are requested by women. In fact, a full 86% of plastic surgery patients are working women. And these procedures are not always done to look younger but many times to deal with side effects of multiple pregnancies and such.

## A Middle-Class Tax in Disguise

*The tax is a middle-class tax in disguise:* Much to my own surprise, according to the American Society of Plastic Surgeons (ASPS) data, 71% of surgeries were for individuals making less than $60,000 a year. These are not people living on Fifth Avenue or in Beverly Hills. According to an ASPS survey, among those planning to have cosmetic procedures within the next two years, 60% reported annual income of $30,000 to $60,000. Only 10% of this group reported income higher than $90,000. The demographics of plastic surgery patients have obviously shifted dramatically over the decades and it is no longer just a "luxury" for the rich and famous. In my own patients, I have many who consider it a necessity to remaining competitive in the workplace.

## Patient Safety and Medical Tourism

*The tax will seriously compromise patient safety and cause increases in unsafe medical tourism:* What most don't know is that the provision is limited to procedures performed by "a licensed medical professional." You can bet that the easiest tax loophole is to seek these procedures from nonmedical personnel in all sorts of inappropriate locations. Already there are problems with complications and even death from cosmetic surgery and procedures performed in salons and by non-qualified personnel. This is such a disastrous consequence and such an obvious one that I would oppose it for that reason alone. Is there such a lack of thoughtfulness about patient safety and the forces that would undermine our efforts to keep patients safe? Additionally, the tax is sure to drive more Americans abroad for these procedures. News programs everywhere have reported on horror stories resulting from medical tourism.

## Not a Success in New Jersey

Why would we mandate a federal tax when it was not a success at a state level in New Jersey? In 2004, New Jersey became the only state to have adopted such a tax. The tax was passed without much discussion of the ramifications and without a cost-benefit analysis to determine the true impact. According to independent studies, for every $1 [New Jersey] collects on the tax, the state loses $3.39 in total revenue. Only a small fraction of the projected revenue has resulted, and there are compelling arguments against it, including the difficulty in collecting it and determining what is taxable. Many patients go out of state now to avoid paying the tax, so New Jersey providers and its economy lose these consumers. Legislation was sponsored to repeal this tax. It passed the [New Jersey] Senate and Assembly in 2006 but was vetoed by Gov. Jon Corzine. Assemblyman Joseph Cryan, who sponsored the legislation and was previously the chairman of the New Jersey Democratic State Committee, has written about the unsuccessful New Jersey experience in a public letter to [Nevada Senator] Harry Reid. Further, at least ten other states have considered this tax and then rejected the idea.

## Cosmetic vs. Reconstructive

*Determining which procedures qualify is tricky:* As evidenced by the New Jersey experience, the distinction between cosmetic and reconstructive procedures is not always clear. It is often difficult to determine which procedures are elective and which are medically necessary. Are we now deferring to tax auditors to determine medical necessity? If you are not clear, consider some of the following procedures that have traditionally been battle areas for patients with insurers and now, apparently, will be up for discussion with tax auditors: breast reductions, some breast reconstructions and symmetry procedures for breast cancer, keloid scars, circumcisions, congenital vascular lesions, benign skin lesions, body contouring after bariatric surgery or massive weight loss, treatment of gynecomastia in men (abnormally large breast tissue), etc.

## Doctors as Tax Collectors

Are doctors expected to act as tax collectors, and what about patient privacy? The provision requires physicians to collect the tax and it then holds physicians liable should an individual fail to pay the tax. This is mandated to be implemented by the beginning of the year.

Do we really want our doctors and their offices to become tax collectors? Additionally, the provision invariably invites the IRS [Internal Revenue Service] into doctors' offices to determine whether procedures are elective or cosmetic. Are they going to look at patient photographs and go through their histories?

The point of all of this is to raise a tiny portion (projected $5.8 billion) of the estimated $848 billion proposed ten-year health care bill. Experience tells me that the total cost will be much higher than projected and the total raised from such a measure will be much less. I hope we all realize that the proposed tax will mainly squeeze the patients (i.e., consumers) and the doctors—not the big pharmaceutical companies. I hope we also realize that at a time when service businesses are hurting, this kind of bill will affect physicians (very small businesses) and their employees, vendors and manufacturers already affected by the economic downturn.

Some proponents argue that these are luxury services and not medical services. I beg to differ. If we commoditize them in this way, then we will see real complications for real people. This is not like getting one's hair colored in a salon—and even if it were, is hair color tax next? Or laser eye surgery? Perhaps a new hip or knee so we can walk better? Where do we draw the line? After all, these are all lifestyle choices and luxuries of one kind or another.

Ultimately, the cosmetic tax is not an effective fund-raising scheme that affects only the privileged few who live on Fifth Avenue and shop on Rodeo Drive. This is a misconception. It will affect mainstream Americans, mainly women with a final cost-benefit analysis that is negative. I have to agree with ASPS president Dr. Michael McGuire, "Medical care should not be used as a tool to fix broken finances."

> "With an ageing, youth-obsessed culture, most surgeons expect to see more men coming in for surgery."

# More Men Get Cosmetic Surgery

*Leah Hardy*

*Leah Hardy is a British health journalist. In the following viewpoint, she insists that the number of men having cosmetic procedures has risen in recent years, especially in the United Kingdom. With increased emphasis on appearance and competition in the workplace, men are lining up for Botox injections, liposuction, and other enhancements, Hardy writes. The increasing number of male patients brings new challenges, the author maintains—conventional face-lifts may feminize the face, and men have thicker skin, leading to more bleeding and greater potential of scarring. But cutting-edge techniques can create a more masculine brow, bigger pectoral muscles, or a larger nose, Hardy claims.*

As you read, consider the following questions:

1. According to the author, by what percentage has the number of men receiving cosmetic surgery increased?

Leah Hardy, "Top Plastic Surgery Procedures for Men," *Times Online*, March 16, 2008. Copyright © 2008 Times Newspapers Ltd. Reproduced by permission.

2. How do male patients deal with the pain of cosmetic surgery differently than females, in the view of Alex Karidis?

3. Where do men choose to have liposuction, as stated by the author?

These days, it's not just women who are opting for a nip or tuck. In the past five years [2003 to 2008], the number of men turning to cosmetic surgery has risen by more than 300%, according to the British Association of Aesthetic Plastic Surgeons (BAAPS).

Figures for men using Botox are even more startling—Patrick Bowler, the medical director of Court House Clinics, says that one in 10 of his Botox clients are now male. And, thanks to the arrival of Dysport, the male Botox injection, these numbers are set to increase again. Dysport does away with the spookily surprised look that isn't quite so fetching on blokes [men], giving a heavier, [British prime minister] Gordon Brown-style brow instead.

Other popular procedures include nose jobs (rhinoplasty), liposuction, eyelid surgery (blepharoplasty), ear correction (otoplasty), face-lifts and neck lifts. In fact, the surgery-lite business is booming. At Court House Clinics, procedures for men, such as silicone calf implants, are given equal billing with those for women. Bowler says: "Tattoo removal, hair restoration, laser hair removal and glycolic skin peels are top of the popularity chart."

Last year [2007], there was a 60% increase in tummy tucks for men, largely as a result of weight loss surgery that sheds the stones and leaves behind excess skin.

It's hard to imagine John Wayne or Jack Nicholson toying with the idea of a spot of lipo and yearning wistfully for a baby-smooth forehead. So, why are so many men resorting to the scalpel—including, it is rumoured, [actor] George Clooney, who made reference to having an eye lift last year?

Rajiv Grover, a consultant plastic surgeon and member of the BAAPS council, attributes the trend to a culture of "facial discrimination". "Not only are men, especially those in high-powered jobs, expected to be eternally youthful in terms of stamina and dynamism, but they are increasingly judged on their looks," he says. "Also, men are realising that problems they thought they were stuck with, such as gynaecomastia [man boobs], are actually treatable."

The surgeon Donato Zizi, who works at the Court House Clinic in London and specialises in hair transplants, puts it more bluntly. "Men are vain, and they are becoming much less self-conscious about procedures," he says.

So, what kind of man has cosmetic surgery? London surgeon Alex Karidis notes that many of his clients are perfectionists. "One guy, an architect, turned up with blueprints for his new nose," he says. "Full-scale drawings, done from different angles and planned to the last millimetre. That made me pretty apprehensive—surgery simply isn't that accurate. But it was okay in the end."

Karidis's experience is not unusual. "Men tend to be less stoical and complain more than women," says Grover. "Men are often more anxious, too, so that might make them more susceptible to pain. They often want more pain relief."

Karidis recalls: "I had a couple who both came in for liposuction. The next day, she was up and about, but he was still lying there and really struggling. That's not unusual. Some men are a bit wussy: They have 'man recovery', in the same way they have 'man flu.'" Some men scar more easily, too. "Men have thicker skin," says Grover. "If it is thinner, you get a finer scar. With facial surgery, the key difficulty is deciding where to hide the scars without hair and makeup to cover them."

Grover sees another problem. "I am cautious about treating men for facial rejuvenation," he says. "In the wrong hands, there is a risk of feminising the face. For example, to support

# Cosmetic Surgery Options for Men

## A manly brow

Dr Nick Lowe is a specialist in Dysport, a form of botulinum toxin different from Botox. According to Lowe, Botox treatment "can look bizarre and feminine on men." Studies show that ovulating women often have a strong preference for "a low pupil-to-brow ratio," which means they find the stern, glowering brows of Gordons Ramsay [celebrity chef] and Brown [British prime minister] more sexually alluring than [Irish television host] Graham Norton-style raised eyebrows.

## The pec injection

Macrolane, a new type of long-lasting filler, makes it possible to have bigger pecs and manlier calves without surgery. Christopher Inglefield, a consultant surgeon at London Bridge Plastic Surgery, is leading clinical research into Macrolane in the UK [United Kingdom]. "I can make small changes to body shape that make a big difference to my patients," he says. The procedure, which takes place under local anaesthetic and has no downtime, involves inserting a cannula tube to push the Macrolane into the right part of the body.

## A bigger nose

A larger nose is an option for men cursed with a cute little button. The method, created by the reconstructive surgeon Martin H Kelly, involves placing a "self-expander," which looks like a thick contact lens, under the skin at the tip of the nose for two weeks. This gradually swells up, allowing the patient to grow extra skin.

*Leah Hardy, "Top Plastic Surgery Procedures for Men,"*
Times Online *(UK), March 16, 2008.*

the lower eyelid during a face-lift on a woman, you might raise the outer corner slightly. This looks attractive, as it creates a nice almond shape, but it wouldn't look good on a man."

Most surgeons agree that face-lifts are harder to do on men. They have a higher incidence of bleeding due to the thickness of the skin and the fact that men are more likely to have high blood pressure than women. They also have a higher infection rate and more swelling.

When it comes to liposuction, men opt to have it on the waist, abdomen and chest, which can cost from £3,000 [$4,600] to £6,000 [$9,300]. The procedure doesn't work for beer bellies, as they are caused by fat underlying the muscle, but it does work for man boobs, something that more than 30% of men have. Treatment involves liposuction to remove excess fat, and then removing the gland under the nipple. It costs about £4,000 [$6,200], and the patient can be back on his feet in a few days.

So, what's the future? With an ageing, youth-obsessed culture, most surgeons expect to see more men coming in for surgery and less furtiveness about booking a fortnight off work to have a spot of lipo or a face-lift. And given the male propensity to boast about just about anything, a new nose or a brow-lift could soon rival the MacBook Air [a notebook computer] in the status stakes.

| "Stem cells can be valuable 'tools' for plastic surgeons and their patients."

# Stem Cells Will Improve Cosmetic Surgery

## Richard Ellenbogen, as told to Connie Jennings

*In the following viewpoint, Richard Ellenbogen and Connie Jennings discuss the potential of using stem cells for facial rejuvenation. Ellenbogen claims that transferring fat, which contains stem cells, to the face tightens and fills the skin for a more youthful appearance. Since the stem cells are collected from the patient, there are very low risks of tissue rejection or complications, he claims. Other benefits of a stem cell face-lift, Ellenbogen upholds, are a more natural look and less invasive surgery at the same cost of a surgical face-lift. Ellenbogen is a plastic surgeon who helped pioneer the cosmetic application of stem cells. Jennings is a contributing writer for* Plastic Surgery Practice *magazine.*

As you read, consider the following questions:

1. In Jenning's view, what are the pluses of stem cells in cosmetic surgery?

2. Why do stem cells act as a "rejuvenator," in the view of Ellenbogen?

3. What is the most common adverse effect of a face-lift using stem cells, as stated by Ellenbogen?

A dult stem cells are found in large quantities in fat cells and act a repairman of sorts. They assist in replenishing specialized cells, such as those lost within the face in the normal process of aging, as well as maintain a normal "turnover" of regenerative organs, such as blood or skin.

Due to these properties, stem cells can be valuable "tools" for plastic surgeons and their patients.

Possible applications include rejuvenation of the skin or recreation of a youthful appearance in a patient's complexion without the need for chemical or laser treatments—a definite plus. A cell that will maintain its shape or form long term, and in fact continue to "graft" with time to an area that has lost either volume or turgor, is another plus.

It is amazing to consider the possibilities now available for facial reconstruction using stem cells harvested from the patient's own body. The client is both donor and recipient, so there is no "rejection" of the tissues or cells, and the result is obviously very natural.

Another point of interest: The stem cells are harvested via liposuction.

There is no complicated procedure for gathering them up or separating them out. It is a matter of simply "spinning them down" after the liposuction, then reinserting them into the desired areas.

## The Stem Cell Facelift

The advances made in plastic surgery techniques using stem cells are perhaps best stated by Richard Ellenbogen, MD, FACS,

FICS. Ellenbogen is widely recognized for his work in using stem cells present in liposuctioned fat for a procedure known as the Stem Cell Facelift.

Considered by many to be the "father of fat grafting," Ellenbogen is a two-time recipient of the American Medical Association Physician's Recognition Award, a member of the American Society of Plastic Surgeons, the American Society for Aesthetic Plastic Surgery, a fellow of the American College of Surgeons, and a fellow of the International College of Surgeons.

"The latest developments in adipose stem cell research were not discovered in a petri dish or in a lab," he says. "Instead, this promising revolution in medicine was inspired via unexpected benefits resulting from facial fat grafting. In fact, it was and is consistently observed that the transplanted fat did not feel like isolated collections of fat, but remarkably, rather more like the recipient-site tissue into which it had been transplanted."

Ellenbogen began his career more than 30 years ago. After attending the University of Florida, where he excelled in both art and premed classes, he obtained his medical degree from the University of Miami. He went on to complete his general surgery training in New York City, where his interest in corrective surgery grew. He traveled to The Hague, Netherlands, where he served as a fellow to the Red Cross Hospital, giving assistance to children with birth defects.

Upon returning to the United States, Ellenbogen moved to Los Angeles and became board certified in plastic surgery. His Beverly Hills practice opened in 1980.

llenbogen also has some experience as a portrait artist, which explains his frequent references to the importance of being able to sculpt and shape the face. Currently, he is a clinical instructor of plastic surgery at the University of Southern California.

## The Natural Course

*[Plastic Surgery Practice:] How did you get involved in stem cell research, and what prompted you to relate that to plastic surgery?*

Richard Ellenbogen: It was the natural course to take, really. My first article on fat grafting was in 1978 in *Modern Plastic Surgery.*

It was only recently that we discovered we were not only grafting fat, but we were also transferring stem cells. We noticed when we transferred the fat, there were a lot of changes in the complexion of the skin. The pores became closer together; the pigmentation was lighter; all the things which are generally done through external means or treatments—creams or chemicals, such as hydrocortisone, Retin-A, and hydroxyl acids. We were seeing very similar effects without applying anything externally to the skin. In fact, what I used to call it before we discovered the stem cells is the "balloon effect." I would put the fat into the face and noticed that the skin would get shinier, and [as] the writing on a balloon gets lighter the pigmentation on the skin would be lighter.

I worked with Dr Peter Rubin from the University of Pittsburgh, who is kind of the "guru" of stem cells. The balloon effect, now known as the Stem Cell Facelift, also causes the pores to become closer, and a tightening of the skin, which in turn creates skin that is more youthful in appearance.

*How are the stem cells placed into the desired areas?*

There are basically two ways to put stem cells into the face. Number one, the liposuctioned stem cells can be separated out of the fat cells and reinjected. There are some Japanese surgeons who have been injecting stem cells mixed with fat cells into breast tissue in order to attempt to "grow" more natural breast tissue.

Unfortunately, to this time, this has not been the case for them or for us as well. Consequently, we feel that possibly it is the separation of the stem cells from the fat cells that decreases their viability. Therefore, it [is] better to do as little extraneously to the stem cells as is necessary for their survival.

*Are there "ideal" sites for liposuctioning the fat cells, or areas in which there is a greater concentration of stem cells present?*

The highest concentration of stem cells is in the back fat, traditionally called the love handles. The stem cells are more stable in these more fibrous areas. . . .

## A Minimalist Approach

*With what ease are these stem cells harvested, and are there any pre-procedural preparations necessary for the client?*

There is no special preparation necessary. There is about a 2-cm [centimeter] incision made into the love handle, and the fat cells are liposuctioned. It is generally well tolerated and heals quickly. Clients are very pleased.

*Is the Stem Cell Facelift a multistep procedure? Do the stem cells need to be separated from the less useful fat tissues/cells prior to being reinjected into the desired regions of the face?*

With research, various options have been tried, and what has been found to be most effective is just to centrifuge the cells. Separating them from the other fat cells tends to decrease their viability, so techniques that involve separating or washing the cells have been abandoned. Instead, a minimalist approach is used in order to maximize the viability of the stem cells. The layer of fat that is centrifuged out is used to correct irregularities and create a well-proportioned face.

## Short- and Long-Term Benefits

*How do the risks and benefits of the Stem Cell Facelift compare to those of a traditional facelift?*

There are no increased risks of Stem Cell Facelift versus traditional. There are, however, a significant number of benefits—both short and long term—to the Stem Cell Facelift.

Injecting the liposuctioned fat, rich with stem cells, into the subcutaneous area requires no lifting of the SMAS

## Plastic Surgery Plays a Central Role in Stem Cell Research

Think of stem cells as your body's way of remaking spare parts in your time of need. This is a slight oversimplification, but the very practical, timely hope for stem cell research is that instead of using synthetics in the future, we can use our own body's cells to regenerate muscles, skin, and even bone.

Although the practical application of stem cell research in plastic surgery and dermatology may still be a few years away, we'll go out on a limb and predict that you'll be seeing these procedures performed within a decade rather than the twenty to twenty-five years that most other researchers claim. The field of plastic surgery is playing a central role in this research.

*Douglas Hamilton and Babak Azizzadeh,*
Beverly Hills Beauty Secrets: A Prominent Dermatologist
and Plastic Surgeon's Insider Guide to Facial Rejuvenation.
*Hoboken, NJ: John Wiley & Sons, 2009.*

(superficial musculoaponeurotic system), but has the same effect as stitching with a traditional facelift. In superficial areas of the cheek, fat grafting is done for symmetry.

Additional injections can be made into the nasolabial folds [laugh lines] and, when injected underneath the eyes they can obviate the need to perform blepharoplasty [eyelid surgery]. It allows for much contouring of the cheeks and under the eyes, as well as under the temporalis muscle.

The "take" of the fat and stem cells is excellent, and there are the added benefits, previously mentioned—of improved pigmentation, closer pores, and a better overall complexion.

Because the stem cells are easily accepted, they act as a rejuvenator to the tissues already there. This results in skin with an overall younger, tighter appearance. The benefits are excellent both long and short term and very rarely need touch-ups.

## Few Issues with Rejection

*What about adverse effects or risk of rejecting the cells?*

There really aren't any issues with rejection. The most common adverse effect would be the potential for "lumpy" areas, subcutaneously, at the injection sites. However, this can be avoided by carefully applied pressure to the areas of injection. We can sculpt/shape the tissue quite vigorously after injection. Again, it allows for a much more natural appearance of the skin through the contouring and shaping of the cells injected.

*Is the cost of a Stem Cell Facelift comparable to that of a traditional facelift, despite the need for the additional lipo procedure?*

The cost is no more than a traditional facelift. The advantage is that with the Stem Cell Facelift, it includes a general tightening of the skin, better overall condition of the skin, and it is a process where we create a different contour and shape of the face. We can give the effect of high cheekbones and blepharoplasty with the fat/stem cell grafting.

## Technique and Philosophy

*How long have you been doing facelifts with fat grafting?*

I have been doing the facelifts with fat grafting for 20 years. Facelift lipo–stem cell injections can be done with or without face lifting, and there are few risks. Actual injections of fat underneath the top layer of subcutaneous tissue lifts the face in a similar way that stitches would in a traditional facelift.

*What, if any, special equipment might be needed to incorporate the Stem Cell Facelift in one's practice?*

It does not require any special equipment, only simple equipment readily available at any medical supply company. The Stem Cell Facelift is more about technique and philosophy.

*How might President [Barack] Obama's efforts to lift restrictions on stem cell research affect your plastic surgery work?*

While the field for embryonic stem cell research is wide open, the possibilities for regrowth of spinal cord, heart disease, and myocardial infarctions are endless. These are the most important things to society. The changes made by the president will not affect the research or use of stem cells in plastic surgery, because "we're just the beauty guys."

# Periodical Bibliography

*The following articles have been selected to supplement the diverse views presented in this chapter.*

| | |
|---|---|
| Steve Almond | "Vanity, Thy Name Is Tax Revenue," *Boston Globe*, November 30, 2009. |
| Josh Barro | "Why Tax Botox?" *Forbes*, December 7, 2009. |
| Martin Donoho | "Women's Health in Context: Cosmetic Surgery Past, Present, and Future: Scope, Ethics, and Policy," Medscape, August 28, 2006. www.medscape.com. |
| Amanda Fortini | "Lines, Please: If You Can't Move Your Face, Can You Still Act with It?" *New York Magazine*, March 7, 2010. |
| Grace Gold | "Online Consultations the Future of Plastic Surgery? Some Doctors Say Yes, Others Worry," Stylist.com, February 2, 2010. www.stylelist.com. |
| Paul Harasim | "'Botax' Could Create a Few More Wrinkles," *Las Vegas Review-Journal*, November 28, 2009. |
| Patrick Range McDonald | "Nip Tuck," *Advocate*, April 8, 2008. |
| Joanna McGarry | "The New Face of Cosmetic Surgery," *Sunday Times* (London), April 11, 2010. |
| N.D. Moscoe and Nicanor Isse | "The Suture of the Future?" *Plastic Surgery Practice*, April 2007. |
| Rochelle Nataloni | "Adipose Stem Cell Developments Overseas Open New Doors for Cosmetic Surgery," *Cosmetic Surgery Times*, August 1, 2010. |
| Patty Reiman | "The Future (and Beauty) of Fat," *New You*, June 23, 2010. |

# For Further Discussion

## Chapter 1

1. Jenny Kleeman maintains that the public's perception of the safety of cosmetic surgery is distorted. Do you agree or disagree with the author? Why or why not?

2. Victoria Corderi argues that traveling abroad to South America for cosmetic surgery is risky. In your opinion, do the precautions for medical tourism that John Otis recommends protect patients? Cite examples from the texts to support your answer.

## Chapter 2

1. In your view, do Richard D'Amico and Sabrina Joseph and Khorally Pierre express any similar concern regarding when a teenager should not have cosmetic surgery? Use examples from the viewpoints to explain your response.

2. Does Amy Wilentz successfully counter the argument that cosmetic surgery preserves ethnic traits? Why or why not?

## Chapter 3

1. Loren Eskenazi is both a practitioner and a patient of cosmetic surgery. In your opinion, does this strengthen her argument that women who choose plastic surgery have deeply personal and profound motivations? Why or why not?

2. Melissa Dittmann proposes that cosmetic surgery may not boost self-esteem but that studies in the area are scarce. In your opinion, does this undermine her position? Use examples from the text to support your response.

3. Amy Larocca insists that cosmetic surgery and treatments

increase the pressure on women to look younger. Do you agree or disagree with the author? Why or why not?

## Chapter 4

1. Claudia Deutsch states that a tax on cosmetic surgery would help end the biased pressure on women to look younger. Does Haideh Hirmand successfully counter this claim? Cite examples from the viewpoint to explain your answer.

2. Do you agree or disagree with Leah Hardy that attitudes of men regarding cosmetic surgery are shifting toward greater acceptance? Use examples from the text to support your response.

# Organizations to Contact

*The editors have compiled the following list of organizations concerned with the issues debated in this book. The descriptions are derived from materials provided by the organizations. All have publications or information available for interested readers. The list was compiled on the date of publication of the present volume; the information provided here may change. Be aware that many organizations take several weeks or longer to respond to inquiries, so allow as much time as possible.*

**American Board of Plastic Surgery Inc. (ABPS)**
Seven Penn Center, Suite 400, 1635 Market Street
Philadelphia, PA   19103-2204
(215) 587-9322
e-mail: info@abplsurg.org
website: www.abplsurg.org

An independent, nonprofit organization, the American Board of Plastic Surgery Inc. (ABPS) aims to promote safe, ethical, efficacious plastic surgery to the public by maintaining high standards for the education, examination, certification, and maintenance of certification of plastic surgeons as specialists and subspecialists. ABPS is one of twenty-four medical specialty boards that make up the American Board of Medical Specialties (ABMS).

**American Psychological Association (APA)**
750 First Street NE, Washington, DC   20002-4242
(800) 374-2721
website: www.apa.org

Based in Washington, D.C., the American Psychological Association (APA) is a scientific and professional organization that represents psychology in the United States. With 150,000 members, APA is the largest association of psychologists worldwide. It publishes articles and reports on beauty, cosmetic surgery, and other related topics in its numerous journals, and its books include *The Psychology of Beauty* and *Exacting Beauty: Theory, Assessment, and Treatment of Body Image Disturbance.*

### American Society for Aesthetic Plastic Surgery (ASAPS)

11262 Monarch Street, Garden Grove, CA 92841
(800) 364-2147 • fax: (562) 799-1098
e-mail: asaps@surgery.org
website: www.surgery.org

Founded in 1967, the American Society for Aesthetic Plastic Surgery (ASAPS) is a professional organization of plastic surgeons who are certified by the American Board of Plastic Surgery Inc. and specialize in cosmetic plastic surgery. With more than two thousand members in the United States, Canada, and many other countries, ASAPS is at the forefront of innovation in aesthetic plastic surgery around the world.

### American Society of Breast Surgeons

5950 Symphony Woods Road, Suite 212
Columbia, MD 21044
(877) 992-5470 • fax: (410) 992-5472
website: www.breastsurgeons.org

The American Society of Breast Surgeons, an organization for general surgeons who treat patients with breast disease, is committed to continually improving the practice of breast surgery by serving as an advocate for surgeons who seek excellence in the care of breast patients. This mission is accomplished by providing a forum for the exchange of ideas and by promoting education, research, and the development of advanced surgical techniques.

### American Society of Plastic Surgeons (ASPS)

444 E. Algonquin Road, Arlington Heights, IL 60005
(847) 228-9900
website: www.plasticsurgery.org

The American Society of Plastic Surgeons (ASPS) is the largest plastic surgery specialty organization in the world. Established in 1931, it offers patients and consumers information on cosmetic and reconstructive surgery procedures, an online database of plastic surgery statistics, and technology briefs on the latest developments and advances in the field.

### Appearance Research Institute (ARI)
e-mail: gordon@gordonpatzer.com
website: www.gordonpatzer.com

Once fully established, the Appearance Research Institute (ARI) will be a multidisciplinary, global, cross-cultural, not-for-profit organization with an emphasis on scientific research and multiple forms of communication to advance the understanding of appearance around the world. The institute is headed by Gordon L. Patzer, author and dean of the Walter E. Heller College of Business Administration at Roosevelt University, and will include a research center, the Center for the Study of Physical Attractiveness (C-SPA); and an outreach arm, the Appearance Phenomenon Association (APA).

### Federal Trade Commission (FTC)
Consumer Response Center, 600 Pennsylvania Avenue NW
Washington, DC   20580
(877) 382-4357
website: www.ftc.gov

The Federal Trade Commission (FTC) deals with issues that touch the economic life of every American. It is the only federal agency with both consumer protection and competition jurisdiction in broad sectors of the economy. The FTC pursues vigorous and effective law enforcement; advances consumers' interests by sharing its expertise with federal and state legislatures and U.S. and international government agencies; develops policy and research tools through hearings, workshops, and conferences; and creates practical and plain-language educational programs for consumers and businesses in a global marketplace with constantly changing technologies. The commission monitors the labeling and advertising claims of beauty and personal care products.

**Food and Drug Administration (FDA)**
10903 New Hampshire Avenue
Silver Spring, MD   20993-0002
(888) 463-6332
website: www.fda.gov

The Food and Drug Administration (FDA) is one of the nation's oldest consumer protection agencies. Its mission is to promote and protect the public health by helping safe and effective products reach the market in a timely way; monitoring products for continued safety after they are in use; and helping the public get the accurate, science-based information needed to improve health. The FDA determines the safety of materials used in cosmetic surgery such as breast implants.

**International Medical Spa Association**
310 Seventeenth Street, Union City, New Jersey   07087
(201) 865-2065 • fax: (201) 865-3961
e-mail: medspaassn@aol.com
website: www.medicalspaassociation.org

The International Medical Spa Association is dedicated to the creation of a positive industry image, and the enhancement of those who serve it, through the development, implementation, and continuous evaluation of a practical, but strict, code of ethics based upon the highest standards of care and regulated peer review. Its members are professionals with health care or spa experience, working together to develop and implement programs that will help shape the future of the medical spa industry.

**Medical Spa Society (MSS)**
e-mail: info@medicalspasociety.com
website: www.medicalspasociety.com

The mission of the Medical Spa Society (MSS) is to promote education, communication, and standards of excellence for the medical spa profession. The society is dedicated to the advancement of the medical spa industry in all aspects, including the interests of members, their staffs, and consumers, with the goal of encouraging the exchange of information and ideas and developing and adhering to high standards of care and a code of ethics. MSS publishes an online newsletter and holds Web seminars for its members.

# Bibliography of Books

Carla Bluhm and
Nathan Clendenin
*Someone Else's Face in the Mirror: Identity and the New Science of Face Transplants.* Westport, CT: Praeger, 2009.

Virginia L. Blum
*Flesh Wounds: The Culture of Cosmetic Surgery.* Berkeley, CA: University of California Press, 2003.

Gregory A.
Buford and
Steven E. House
*Beauty and the Business: Practice, Profits and Productivity, Performance and Profitability.* Garden City, NY: Morgan James Publishing, 2010.

Anthony Elliott
*Making the Cut: How Cosmetic Surgery Is Transforming Our Lives.* London, UK: Reaktion Books, 2008.

Susan Whitman
Helfgot
*The Match: Complete Strangers, a Miracle Face Transplant, Two Lives Transformed.* New York: Simon & Schuster, 2010.

Geoffrey Jones
*Beauty Imagined: A History of the Global Beauty Business.* New York: Oxford University Press, 2010.

Susan E. Kolb
*The Naked Truth About Breast Implants: From Harm to Healing: A Spiritual Healer's Journey as a Plastic Surgeon.* Savage, MN: Lone Oak Publishing, 2010.

Alex Kuczynski
*Beauty Junkies: Inside Our $15 Billion Obsession with Cosmetic Surgery.* New York: Doubleday, 2006.

Cap Lesesne      *Confessions of a Park Avenue Plastic Surgeon.* New York: Gotham Books, 2005.

Carol M. Martin      *The Little Book of Lipo: Everything You Need to Know About Liposuction but Didn't Know to Ask.* Atlanta, GA: Busystreet Press, 2007.

Suellen May and David J. Triggle      *Botox and Other Cosmetic Drugs.* New York: Chelsea House, 2008.

Rhian Parker      *Women, Doctors and Cosmetic Surgery: Negotiating the "Normal" Body.* New York: Palgrave Macmillan, 2010.

Gordon L. Patzer      *The Power and Paradox of Physical Attractiveness.* Boca Raton, FL: BrownWalker Press, 2006.

Arthur W. Perry      *Straight Talk About Cosmetic Surgery.* New Haven, CT: Yale University Press, 2007.

Katherine A. Phillips      *Understanding Body Dysmorphic Disorder: An Essential Guide.* New York: Oxford University Press, 2009.

Victoria Pitts-Taylor      *Surgery Junkies: Wellness and Pathology in Cosmetic Culture.* New Brunswick, NJ: Rutgers University Press, 2007.

Jeff Schult      *Beauty from Afar: The Medical Tourist's Guide to Affordable and Quality Cosmetic Surgery Outside the United States.* New York: Stewart, Tabori & Chang, 2006.

Maria Siemionow    *Face to Face: My Quest to Perform the First Full Face Transplant.* New York, Kaplan Publishing, 2009.

Margot Starbuck    *Unsqueezed: Springing Free from Skinny Jeans, Nose Jobs, Highlights and Stilettos.* Downers Grove, IL: IVP Books, 2010.

Arlene Weintraub    *Selling the Fountain of Youth: How the Anti-Aging Industry Made a Disease Out of Getting Old—And Made Billions.* New York: Basic Books, 2010.

# Index

## A

Aboolian, Andre, 18
Actors. *See* Entertainment industry
Adams, Jan, 18, 21–22, 23
Addiction to surgery, 97, 108
Advertising
    surgical procedures, 27
    word-of-mouth, 35, 42–43
Advertising Standards Authority
    (United Kingdom), 27
Aesthetic Anthropology Survey of
    Beauty and Grooming Across
    Cultures, 123, 125, 127
African Americans. *See* Ethnic
    characteristics
Aging
    combating, via surgery, 86, 90,
        97, 113–120, 122–123
    denial, 115–116, 118–119
    gender double standards, 89–
        90, 137, 139–140
    surgery to look good for one's
        age, 121–127
Alcohol and drug dependence
    deaths, 76, 78
American Board of Plastic Sur-
    gery, 57
American Society of Plastic Sur-
    geons
    taxation opinions, 139, 143,
        146
    teen surgery opinions, 53, 55
    travel/tourism surgery opin-
        ions, 37–38, 43–44
Anesthesia
    mistakes, 44

    risk, 56
Argentina, 34, 36
    *See also* Tourism
Armani, Antonio, 129
Arndt, Kenneth A., 77
Asia, 37, 41
    *See also* China; Tourism
Asians and Asian-Americans. *See*
    Ethnic characteristics
Azizzadeh, Babak, 157

## B

Bacteria-related complications,
    44–45
Bainbridge, Pauline, 26, 28–30
Batt, Lorraine, 31
Beam, Christopher, 138
Beauty pageants, 36
Beauty standards
    beauty and fashion industries
        as drivers, 64, 71, 73, 118
    breast size, 61–62, 89
    Caucasian looks and Western
        standards, 51–52, 64, 65–73
    children, 94–95
    entertainment industry as
        driver, 64, 70, 72–73
    men, 149–151
    professional success and, 128,
        129
    regional standards, 70, 122
    relaxing/changing, 121, 124–
        125
    surgery potential as driver, 86
    universal preferences, 122, 130
    unrealistic, 89, 90
Blepharoplasty. *See* Eyelid surgery

Body dysmorphic disorder, 110–111

Body image
disorders, 78, 88, 110–111
dissatisfaction, 110

Body/mind dichotomy, 87, 97–98, 116

Borud, Loren, 44, 46

Botox
celebrity users, 15, 81
effects, 15, 113, 114, 123, 125, 126
history of use, 14–15, 125
men, 148
public opinion and growth, 14, 15, 69, 105, 121, 123, 126
safety concerns, 15–16

Botulinum toxin type A. *See* Botox

Botulism, 14

Brazil, 34, 36, 37
*See also* Tourism

Breast implants/augmentation
mental health issues and suicide risks, 74, 75–76, 78, 109
popularity and growth rates, 61, 85, 100, 105
risks and side effects, 62–63, 76
self-esteem improvements, 99, 100, 101, 102–103
teenagers, 55, 59, 60, 61–63

Breast reconstruction, 55, 60, 61, 84, 145

Breast reduction surgeries
cosmetic vs. reconstructive debate, 145
fatalities, 18, 27
teenagers, 55

Brow surgery (men), 147, 148, 150

Brown, Adrienne, 27

Brumberg, Joan Jacobs, 90

**C**

Calf implants, 148, 150

California Health and Beauty, 20–24

Cancer, breast implants, and reconstruction, 60, 63, 76, 84, 145

Career advancement, 15, 128, 129, 131–132

Carruthers, Jean, 14–15

Castle, David, 106, 108, 112

Caucasian looks and beauty standards, 51–52, 64, 65–71, 73

Celebrity doctors, 21–22, 23, 45, 70

Celebrity magazines and blogs, 81–82, 87, 89
*See also* Entertainment industry

Certification and credentials
consumer research, 21–23, 43, 46, 47, 57
cosmetic surgery tourism, 34, 36–38, 40, 47
practitioners lacking, 21–22, 47

Chan, Steven, 31–32

Chen, William P., 51–52

China, 70, 94–95

Clooney, George, 148

Clothing
coaching and makeovers, 96, 131
styles and age-appropriateness, 114, 118

Colombia, 34, 35–36, 37, 38–39
*See also* Tourism

Complications from surgery. *See* Safety issues

Consumer incomes, 138, 139, 141, 143

Consumer research
availability, 85, 127
doctor choices, 21–23, 42, 43, 46, 47, 57
facilities, 57

Contreras, Edgar, 45–47

Corderi, Victoria, 40–48

Corzine, Jon, 144

Cosmetic Botox. *See* Botox

Costs of surgery, 132
breast implants, 35, 41, 61
eyelid surgery, 51, 132
taxation: con- stance, 141–146
taxation: pro- stance, 137–140
tourism-level rates, 35, 36, 40, 41, 42–43

Counseling
breast implant patients, 78
self-esteem issues, 57, 102
weight issues, 55–56

Credentials, doctors'. *See* Certification and credentials

Cryan, Joseph, 144

Culp, Connie, 135

**D**

D'Amico, Richard, 18, 53–58

Dangers. *See* Safety issues

*Dateline* (NBC News program), 42, 46–47

Death. *See* Fatalities, surgery

Dental treatments, 131, 132

Deutsch, Claudia, 137–140

Diamond, Howard, 70–71

Dittman, Melissa, 104–112

Doctor-patient relationships, 23, 24, 38, 77

Doctor qualifications. *See* Certification and credentials

Dominican Republic, 40, 41–43, 44–47
*See also* Tourism

Donda West Law (California, 2009), 18

Donley-Hayes, Karen, 93–98

Double eyelids. *See* Eyelid surgery

Dover, Jeffrey S., 77

Drug and alcohol dependence deaths, 76, 78

Dweck, Jessica, 137–140

Dysport, 16, 148, 150

**E**

Earning potential, post-surgery, 15, 97–98, 128–132, 149

Ellenbogen, Richard, 152–159

Elliott, Anthony, 94, 95–96, 97–98

Entertainment industry
beauty standard setter, 64, 72–73
consumers of cosmetic surgery, 15–16, 81–82, 89, 148
promoter of surgeries, 21–22, 25, 26, 70, 83, 87, 96, 105

Eskenazi, Loren, 83–92

Ethnic characteristics
Asian eyes and eyelid surgery, 51–52, 66
politics of appearance, 66–67, 68, 73
should be considered prior to surgery, 64–73
surgery in history, 67–68

Ethnic revision, 66, 69–72, 73

European skin care and attitudes, 123, 124, 125, 126, 127

Exercise

benefits, 117, 121
presence in culture, 114, 116, 117–118, 125
surgery vs., 38, 55, 56
*Extreme Makeover* (reality television program), 21, 70, 87, 96, 105
Eye disorders, 14–15, 125
Eyelid surgery
    alternatives, 157
    Asian-American choices and pressures, 51–52
    Asian and Western looks, 66
    costs, 132
    men, 128, 148
    professional motivations, 128, 130–131, 132

**F**

Face transplants, 135–136
Facial surgery
    aging gracefully, 121–127
    combating aging, 113, 114–120, 126–127
    fatalities, 30–31
    makeovers and extreme surgery, 87, 105
    men, 124–125, 128, 130–131, 132, 147, 148, 150–151
    overseas prices, 35, 36, 41
    professional motivations, 128, 130–131, 132
    stem cells use, 152–159
    teenagers, 55, 56
    Western beauty standards and ethnic looks, 51–52, 64, 65–73
    *See also* specific features
Fashion industry, 64, 71, 73, 118
    *See also* Clothing

Fat injections, 81, 126, 152, 153–158
Fatalities, surgery
    incidents, 18, 21, 26, 27, 28–31, 45, 47, 54
    risks, 25, 27, 32–33
    tourism deaths, 45, 47
Federation of State Medical Boards, 23
Figueroa-Haas, Cynthia, 100, 101–102
Fitness. *See* Exercise
Food and Drug Administration (FDA)
    Botox approval, 15, 16, 123, 125–126
    breast implant opinions, 55, 61, 109
    fillers approval, 126

**G**

Gan, Dina, 51
Gastric bypass surgery, 36
Gender and aging: double standards, 89–90, 137, 139–140
Generational differences, 116, 118–119
German history, 67–68
Gilman, Sander, 67–68, 122, 123, 124–125, 126
Globalization, 36, 93, 94, 95, 122
Goldsmith, Olivia, 27
Graf, Jeannette, 115
Grover, Rajiv, 149, 151
Gynecomastia, 55, 145, 149

**H**

Hair transplants, 128, 129, 130, 148, 149
Hamilton, Douglas, 157

Hand transplants, 136
Hardy, Leah, 147–151
Hari, Johann, 15–16
Harley Medical Group, 27
Hartmann, Margaret, 81
Healing, 84, 90–91
    *See also* Recovery processes
Health care reform bills, 137, 138,
    139, 141, 142
Health insurance, 35, 86
Heart conditions and attacks
    complications pre- and post-
    surgery, 26, 27, 28, 30, 45
    consideration, wellness for
    surgery, 18
Heart injuries, post-surgery, 30–31
Hendry, Denise, 32
Hirmand, Haideh, 141–146
Hollywood. *See* Entertainment in-
    dustry
Home improvement television
    shows, 96
Honigman, Roberta, 106

**I**

*I Want a Famous Face* (reality
    television program), 87, 105
Incidence and growth of surgery
    breast implants, 61, 85, 100
    ethnic revision, 69–70
    global, 70, 95
    mainstream inclusion, 15, 70,
    87
    men, 148
    social and cultural pressures,
    93–98, 112, 131
    U.S. statistics, 68–69, 85, 105,
    138
Incomes, surgery consumers, 138,
    139, 141, 143

Infection-related complications,
    28, 44, 62, 151
Inglefield, Christopher, 150
Injectables. *See* Botox; Dysport;
    Fat injections; Juvéderm; Resty-
    lane
Internet research, 85
    breast implants, 63
    doctors and practitioners, 23,
    42

**J**

Jackson, Michael, 66, 73
Jaw surgeries, 30–31
Jennings, Connie, 152–159
Jewish characteristics, 67, 68, 73
Joseph, Jacques, 67, 68, 73
Joseph, Sabrina, 59–63
Juvéderm, 16, 123, 126

**K**

Kaminer, Michael S., 77
Karidis, Alex, 149
Katz, Beth, 61–62
Kelly, Martin H., 150
Kerner, Justinus, 14
Kleeman, Jenny, 25–33

**L**

Lai, Alyssa, 51
Larocca, Amy, 113–120
Latinos. *See* Ethnic characteristics
Lawsuits, 31, 70
Lee, Charles, 66
Lepri, Isabella, 124
Lewis, Wendy, 121–127
Liposuction
    celebrity users, 81

fatalities, 18, 21, 26, 27, 28–30, 45, 54

growth rates, 85, 105

men, 148, 149, 151

near-fatalities, 32

stem cell gathering, 153, 155–156

surgery tourism, 35, 38, 40, 41, 42, 43, 46

teenagers, 55–56

Lipworth, Loren, 75–76, 78

Lowe, Nick, 150

Lung-related complications, 45, 54

**M**

Macrolane, 150

Makeover culture, 41, 70, 81, 93, 94, 96

See also Television promotion of surgery

Malpractice claims

examples, 21, 40

reporting, 46

researching, 23, 47

Mapes, Diane, 14

Maradona, Diego, 36

Marsek, Patrick W., 37

McGee, Micki, 96

McGuire, Michael, 146

Media portrayals of cosmetic procedures

advertising, surgical procedures, 27

Botox as common, 15

surgery as common/mainstream, 26, 61, 70, 83, 87

talk show doctors, 21–22, 23

television promotion of surgery, 21–22, 25, 26, 70, 83, 87, 96, 105

Medical examination and history

failures to collect, 18, 46

guideline/importance, 20, 23–24, 57

office behavior, psychological consideration, 77

Men

aging double standards, 89–90, 137, 139–140

increasing as surgery consumers, 147–151

influence over surgery, 54, 57, 124–125

professional motivations for surgery, 128, 129–132, 147

sexuality, 101–102

Middle Easterners. See Ethnic characteristics

Miller, Oliver, 81–82

Mills, Alexandra, 30–31

Mind/body dichotomy, 87, 97–98, 116

Misra, V. Peter, 15

Mitchell, Deborah, 14

Money. See Costs of surgery; Earning potential, post-surgery; Incomes, surgery consumers

Montag, Heidi, 81, 82

More than Skin Deep: Exploring the Real Reasons Why Women Go Under the Knife (Eskenazi), 83–92

Morel, Maria, 41, 43, 45, 47, 48

Motherhood, 118, 119

Multicultural beauty standards, 64, 66, 72–73

See also Ethnic characteristics

## N

Nassif, Paul, 65, 71
National beauty standards, 70
National Health Service (United Kingdom), 27
Nauert, Rick, 99–103
New Jersey, tax policy, 142–143, 144–145
Newsmax.com, 74–78
Nose jobs. *See* Rhinoplasty
Nurses, 38, 43, 77, 102–103

## O

Obasanjo, Stella, 27
Office behavior observation, 77
Otis, John, 34–39

## P

Parent-teen relations, 56–57, 58, 114
"Passing" (racial), 66–67, 68
Patzer, Gordon, 130, 131, 132
Pectoral injections, 150
*People* (magazine), 81, 87
"Perfection" desires, 81, 86, 149
Phillips, Katharine, 106
Physician qualifications. *See* Certification and credentials
Pierre, Khorally, 59–63
Politics of appearance, 66–67, 68, 73
Preoperative consultations
    behavior observation and psychological screening, 74, 77, 78, 107, 110–111
surgery tourism, 36–37, 43, 46
teens, 53, 56–58
*See also* Consumer research; Medical examination and history
Procedure descriptions, 38–39, 44
Professional motivations for surgery, 15, 97–98, 128–132, 149
*Psychological Aspects of Reconstructive and Cosmetic Plastic Surgery: Clinical, Empirical and Ethical Perspectives* (Sarwer), 111
Psychological health
    consideration, teen cosmetic surgery, 55–56, 62, 110
    exercise and, 117–118
    not studied/considered enough with surgery, 83, 85, 86–87, 88–91, 106, 110, 112
    office behavior observation, 77
    self-esteem boosts from breast surgery, 99, 100, 101, 102–103
    self-esteem not necessarily improved with surgery, 104, 105–112
    surgery candidates should be screened, 74–78, 102, 104, 107, 110–111
    surgery inappropriateness cases, 88–89, 102, 108, 110–111
Public opinion
    Botox, 14, 15, 69, 105, 121, 123, 126
    cosmetic surgery, 25, 85–86, 127

judgments of consumers, 81–82, 86–87, 102–103

**R**

Reality television. *See* Television promotion of surgery
Reconstructive surgeries
  descriptions, 60, 84, 135
  difference from cosmetic, 54, 60, 88, 138, 141, 144–145
  face transplants, 135–136
  teenagers, 55, 59, 61
Recovery processes, 91
  avoiding, via injectables, 123
  examples, 39
  men, 149
  time commitment, 54
  underestimated/downplayed, 87–88
Restylane, 16
Rhinoplasty
  costs, 132
  ethnic characteristic retention, 71–72, 73
  history, 67, 68
  men, 124–125, 148, 150
  teenagers, 55, 56
  Western/white beauty standards, 65–66, 70–71
Rites of passage, 83, 90, 91–92
Rivers, Joan, 82
Rosenberg Self-Esteem Scale, 101
Rossum, Emmy, 81
Rubin, Peter, 155

**S**

Safety issues
  consumer research, 21–23, 42, 43, 46, 47, 57, 127

cosmetic surgery is dangerous, 25–33
cosmetic surgery is safe, 20–24
cosmetic surgery tourism is dangerous, 40–48, 143–144
cosmetic surgery tourism is safe, 34–39
hospitalization from complications, 26, 27–28, 29, 44, 46, 57
legislation promoting safety, 18–19
nature of surgery, 91
risks minimized, 27, 83, 87–88
surgery errors and complications, 30–31, 44–45
teen surgery, 56, 110
*See also* Fatalities, surgery
Sarwer, David B., 78, 107–108, 109, 110–111
Scarring, 67–68, 87, 91, 126, 149
Schwarzenegger, Arnold, 18
Scott, Alan B., 14–15
Screening of patients. *See* Medical examination and history; Preoperative consultations; Psychological health
Sebagh, Jean-Louis, 15
Segura, Allyn, 41, 43, 44, 45
Self-esteem
  consideration for teen surgery, 53, 54–55, 56–57, 62
  exercise and, 117
  measurement methods, 101
  racial identity and, 66–67
  relevance in adult surgery desires, 41, 83, 87, 89, 90, 92, 102
  relevance in teen surgery desires, 60, 62, 63

surgery can improve, 99–103, 107–108
surgery may not improve, 104–112
Sexual confidence and satisfaction, 99, 100, 101
Shah, Darshan, 21–23
Shooting victims, 135
Shulman, Alexandra, 108
Shulman, Matthew, 53–58
Siemionow, Maria, 135
Silicone breast implants, 61, 109
Sims, Josh, 136
"Sin" taxes, 138, 139
Social pressures
    entertainment world, 81–82
    surgery in modern world, 93–98, 112, 131
    taxation of surgery, effects, 137
    See also Beauty standards
South American surgeries. See Tourism
Spear, Scott, 43–44, 48
Stem cell research, 157, 159
Stem cells, in facial surgery, 152–159
Stiles, DeLisa, 105
Suicide risks, 74, 75–76, 76, 78, 109
Surgery procedures. See Incidence and growth of surgery; Procedure descriptions
The Swan (reality television program), 87, 105
Syphilis, 68

T

Tamayo, Yvonne, 41, 43, 44, 45
Taxation

cosmetic surgery should be taxed, 137–140
cosmetic surgery should not be taxed, 141–146
New Jersey policy, 142–143, 144–145
Technological advances
    create cultural surgery pressures, 86, 90, 93, 94, 95, 97–98, 131
    face transplants, 135–136
    history of surgery, 67–68, 126
    stem cell research, 157, 159
Teenagers
    cosmetic surgery can benefit, 53–58
    eyelid surgery, 51
    maturity levels, 54, 56, 58, 59, 62
    should not have cosmetic surgery, 59–63
    surgery types and totals, 110, 138
Teeth whitening, 131, 132
Television investigations of surgery tourism, 42, 46–47
Television promotion of surgery, 21–22, 25, 26, 70, 83, 87, 96, 105
Thorpe, Susan, 110
Tourism
    cosmetic surgery tourism is dangerous, 40–48, 143–144
    cosmetic surgery tourism is safe, 34–39
Training, doctor. See Certification and credentials
Transplants. See Face transplants; Hair transplants; Hand transplants
Transracial beauty standards, 64, 66, 72–73

*See also* Ethnic characteristics

**U**

United Kingdom
    advertising, 27
    health services, 27–28
    men's cosmetic surgery, 147,
        148, 149–151

**V**

Vacations
    cultural differences, 124
    surgery tourism as, 35, 38, 39
Vanderbilt, Consuelo, 126
Vanity stereotypes, 83, 87, 89, 90,
    102–103, 125
Vanity taxes. *See* Taxation

**W**

Wells, James, 18–19
West, Donda, 18–19, 21, 27
West, Kanye, 18, 21, 27

Western beauty standards, 51–52,
    64, 65–73
Whitney, Simon, 135–136
Wilentz, Amy, 64–73
Williams, Patricia J., 67
Wilmoth, Sonia, 41, 46
Wolgemuth, Liz, 128–132
Women's sexuality, 101–102
Wong, Martin, 51
Word-of-mouth referrals, 35,
    42–43
Wrinkle treatments, 113, 114–115,
    120, 121, 123–124, 125–127
    *See also* Botox; Dysport; Juvé-
        derm; Restylane
Wyatt, Lance, 72

**Y**

Yesquen, Monica, 35, 38–39

**Z**

Zuckerman, Diana, 106–107, 109,
    110